SPECIAL EDUCATIONAL NEEDS

SPECIAL EDUCATIONAL NEEDS
A RESOURCE FOR PRACTITIONERS

Michael Farrell

Paul Chapman Publishing

Paul Chapman Publishing
A SAGE Publications Company
1 Olivers Yard
London
EC1Y 1SP

SAGE Publications Inc
2455 Teller Road
Thousand Oaks, California 91320

SAGE Publications India Pvt Ltd
B-42 Panchsheel Enclave
Post Box 2109
New Delhi 110 017

Library of Congress Control Number: 2003109189

A catalogue record for this book is available from the
British Library

ISBN 0 7619 4237 8
ISBN 0 7619 4238 6 (pbk)

Typeset by Pantek Arts Ltd, Maidstone, Kent
Printed in Great Britain by T.J. International Ltd,
Padstow, Cornwall

Contents

About the author

Dr Michael Farrell trained as a teacher and as a psychologist at the Institute of Psychiatry and has worked as a headteacher, a lecturer at the Institute of Education, London, and a local authority education inspector. He managed national projects both for City University and for the Department for Education.

Michael Farrell presently works as a special education consultant. This has included policy development and training with local education authorities, work with voluntary organisations, support to schools in the independent and maintained sectors, and advice to the State Bureau of Foreign Experts, China, and the Ministry of Education, Seychelles. He has lectured widely in the UK and abroad.

Author of many articles on education and psychology, he has edited or written thirty educational books, including:

The Handbook of Education (Blackwell, 1996) with Kerry and Kerry
Key Issues for Primary Schools (Routledge, 1999)
Key Issues for Secondary Schools (Routledge, 2001)
Standards and Special Educational Needs (Continuum, 2001)
The Special Education Handbook (David Fulton, 1997; 1998; 2000; 2002)
Understanding Special Educational Needs: A Guide for Student Teachers (Routledge, 2003).

Acknowledgements

I am grateful to the following for reading the manuscript: Dr Derrick Armstrong, Reader in Education, University of Sheffield; Dr Jennifer Evans, Senior Lecturer in Education, School of Educational Foundations and Policy Studies, Institute of Education, London University; Dr Felicity Fletcher-Campbell, Senior Research Officer, National Foundation of Educational Research; Ms Lyn Hurst, headteacher, Heathfield Nursery and Infant School, Twickenham; Dr Tony Lingard, Head of Learning Support, Cambourne Science and Community College, Cornwall; Ms Maria Mole, teacher, Heathfield Nursery and Infant School, Twickenham; Ms Hilary Shand, Special Educational Needs Manager, Reading Borough Council; Professor Sally Tomlinson, research associate, Department of Educational Studies, University of Oxford.

Regarding individual chapters, I am grateful to the following for their comments: for Chapter 3, Mr Simon Oliver, QC, Guildford Chambers, Surrey; Chapter 4, Ms Rosemary Eaton, education consultant; Chapters 6 and 8, Dr Ellie Lee, Department of Sociology and Social Policy, University of Southampton; Chapter 9, Mr Gerry Ackroyd, consultant educational psychologist, London; Chapter 10, Mr Andrew Taylor, SEN Rights and Guidance Team, DfES, London; Chapter 11, Mr Azhar Mobin, Head of LEA Division, Cambridge Education Associates, Cambridge; Chapter 12, Mr John Hattersley, Inclusion Facilitator, Cheshire LEA.

I am grateful to the following for information: Ms Nadia Cole, Project Officer, Education and Social Policy, Local Government Association, London; Mr Paul Fisher, Head of Education Finance and Information and Communications Technology Services, Norfolk LEA; Mr David Jones, headteacher, Riverside School, Hants; Ms Claire Kirby, Statistics Division, Department of Health; Mr Mike McCormack, Senior Inspector SEN, Croydon LEA; Ms Jan Martin, Head of Inclusion and Pupil Support, Northamptonshire LEA; Dr Roger Norgate, consultant educational psychologist, Hampshire LEA; Mr Rob Thompson, headteacher, Henry Tyndale School, Hants; Ms Christine Van-Schagen, SEN Division, DfES; and Dr Ron Weinstein, Clinical Director, The ADD and Family Support Centre.

The assistance of these colleagues does *not* imply that their views are the same as those expressed in the text. The opinions expressed in *Special Educational Needs* are entirely my own, as are any shortcomings of the book.

The support of the staff at Paul Chapman publishing was unstinting and I am particularly grateful to Ms Marianne Lagrange, commissioning editor, education, and to Ms Saleha Nessa, assistant editor, for their help and encouragement.

This book is dedicated to the Reverend Susan Bull
with affection and admiration

1

Introduction

This book is for practitioners, in particular for:

- teachers
- special educational needs co-ordinators
- headteachers, and
- local education authority officers.

Chapters 2–9 seek to illustrate the contribution of a range of different disciplines (history, law, politics, ethics, economics, medicine, sociology and psychology) to aspects of special education. It is hoped that this will encourage any practitioners who may take a view predominantly informed by any one discipline, such as psychology, to explore the contribution of these diverse disciplines to special education.

Chapters 10–12 concern, respectively, national, local and school administrative frameworks for SEN considered particularly in terms of government legislation and guidance. At a national level, the concentration is on organisations, such as the Department for Education and Skills and on guidance. Locally, the focus is organisations such as the LEA as part of the structure along with the procedures and practices normally adopted. Regarding school level structures, particular attention is paid to SEN policy, and to flexibility in the curriculum, assessment and school organisation. The focus in these chapters is maintained primary and secondary mainstream schools in England.

The structure of the book

Chapter 2 outlines the milestones in the history of special education, particularly in England. It also considers changes in terminology, the notion of special education as progress, the motives of special educators and communication approaches to the education of deaf children.

Chapter 3 examines the relationships between the legal definition of SEN, attempts by LEAs to develop local criteria for SEN and the work of the SEN and Disability Tribunal. In relation to current practice, the chapter identifies the conflict between the tribunal's individual case approach and the approach of LEAs in allocating funds for broad areas of SEN. Chapter 4 discusses those things that are important when making political judgements about the future role of local special schools. It explores the concepts of social justice, equal opportunity and discrimination, and considers trends in inclusion that attempt to maintain a balance of pupils in maintained and special schools. Chapter 5, considers the arguments for and against genetic screening and discusses whether such medical procedures devalue the lives of existing disabled people. It then briefly outlines other controversial treatments for children with SEN.

Chapter 6 considers the economic issues involved in special education. It goes onto discuss whether certain conditions (taking the examples of dyslexia and autistic spectrum disorder) which are difficult to define pressurise an essentially redistributive society for more funding. In outlining the importance of local agreements on how SEN is to be identified, assessed and provided for, the chapter goes on to outline a recommended approach to SEN funding and offers suggestions for how local agreements for SEN funding can minimise economic distortions.

Chapter 7 introduces the main elements of a medical model of special education. The chapter considers some of the criticisms of the medical model by looking at an example of a classification of mental disorders that is used to identify learning difficulties and disabilities. Finally, the chapter considers a contemporary approach to special education that seeks to synthesise the medical and social models by identifying the extent of medical and/or social influences on individual and to take action accordingly. Chapter 8 discusses sociological influences on special education, in particular such approaches as structural-functionalist and social constructionist. After briefly noting some common elements of more recent sociological approaches to SEN, the chapter looks at some of the potential difficulties of a sociological perspective. It then considers the current contribution of sociological influences to the *Special Educational Needs Code of Practice* (DfES, 2001a), the notion of 'barriers to learning', understandings of physical disability and interactionist approaches to SEN.

Chapter 9 examines psychological and other approaches to teaching and learning, such as cognitive-behavioural methods. It then considers such teaching approaches as that outlined by Hay McBer (2000) and looks at the *National Special Educational Needs Specialist Standards* (Teacher Training Agency, 1999). It emphasises the importance of ensuring that such approaches are practicable and are in tune with the requirements of whole classes while, at the same time, providing for individual pupils with SEN. The chapter goes on to suggest that aspects of various contemporary approaches can be used to seek this balance, in particular the National Literacy Strategy (DfEE, 1998a), the National Numeracy Strategy (DfEE, 1999a) and the Key Stage 3 strategy relating to literacy and numeracy (DfEE, 2001a; 2001b).

Finally, the chapter discusses the organisational aspects involved in providing for the learning needs of diverse pupil populations. National frameworks for SEN, in the form of national organisations or parts of them (such as the DfES's SEN Division), and the guidance such bodies produce, are discussed in Chapter 10. Particular attention is paid to the *Special Educational Needs Code of Practice* (DfEs, 2001a) and to *Inclusive Schooling* (DfES, 2001e). It is suggested that further clarity is required regarding a graduated approach to SEN provision and individual SEN and for parental preferences for mainstream or special schools.

Chapter 11 considers the role of the modern LEA and possible future developments, looking specifically at how LEAs can offer support for school improvement. The chapter then examines the links between LEAs and other bodies, such as health and social services, learning and skills councils, voluntary bodies and the private sector. In discussing those developments that have contributed to the need for closer liaison, the chapter goes on to consider Excellence in Cities, Sure Start, Schools Plus and SEN regional partnerships. Finally, Chapter 12, sets out what might be required in a school's SEN policy document. It then looks at the key roles of the governors, the staff, SENCOs and teaching assistants in providing for SEN. The roles and responsibilities of parents are also examined. The chapter then considers the curriculum and school organisation with a view to including a wider range of pupils. In the context of mainstream schools the chapter finally examines the curriculum, assessment and school organisation in terms of both flexibility and differentiation.

2

Historical Dimensions

Introduction

This chapter examines current issues that have an important historical dimension. These are changes in terminology; the notion of special education as progress; the motives of special educators; and forms of communication in the education of deaf children. The chapter also outlines the milestones in the history of special education, particularly in England.

Issues in special education

Changes in terminology

The terminology that was current in earlier centuries now seems archaic and even offensive if it is not understood in the context of the times in which it was used. Institutions for the blind provided for those who were 'industrious', as in the Asylum for the Industrious Blind which opened in Edinburgh in 1765, or those who were poor and needy, as in the Schools for the Indigent Blind founded in Liverpool (1791), London (1800) and Norwich (1805). The terms, 'idiot', 'feeble-minded' and 'imbecile' were widely and officially used. Asylums for 'idiots' opened in Highgate, London (1847), and Colchester (1859), while the Darenth School (1878) provided for 'imbeciles'. A residential school for the 'feeble-minded' opened in Sandlebridge (Cheshire) in 1902.

Official reports and Acts of Parliament employed similar terminology. The Idiots Act was passed in 1886 allowing existing institutions to admit 'idiot children' at their parents' wish. The Egerton Commission (1889), as well as reporting on the blind and the deaf and dumb, also made recommendations for idiots, imbeciles and the feeble-minded. It was as late as 1945 that *The Handicapped Pupils and School Health Service Regulations* replaced the term 'mentally defective' with the expression, 'educationally subnormal'. While the expression 'educationally subnormal' now seems dated, the shift from

'mentally defective' to 'educationally subnormal' was substantial and important, signalling a recognition that the focus was no longer excessively on the
defectiveness of the child but on his or her (statistically) below-normal performance in education.

So far as physical disability was concerned, the terms 'cripple' and 'physically defective' were used as in the Cripples Home and Industrial School for
Girls (1851) in Marylebone and in the Lord Mayor Treloar Cripples Hospital
and College, Alton, Hampshire (1908). The Cripples Training College, which
opened in Leatherhead in 1934, later became the Queen Elizabeth's Training
College for the Disabled. Again, it was as late as 1945 that *The Handicapped
Pupils and School Health Service Regulations* used the term 'physically handicapped' instead of the expression 'physically defective'.

In 1978, the Warnock Report (DES, 1978) proposed that previous categories of handicap should be replaced by the concept of 'special educational
need'. However, only a decade later it was suggested that the concept had
already outlived its usefulness (Pumfrey and Mittler, 1989). More recent suggestions that language such as 'SEN' should be abolished are not, it is
claimed, to do with political correctness but about the use of words that
'create and maintain mind-sets that perpetuate segregation' (Mittler, 2000:
8). In the context of moving towards creating a more inclusive education
system, the continued use of the term 'special' is seen as both anachronistic
and 'discriminatory' (ibid.). Children with SEN, it is argued, are only special
because 'so far the education system has not been able to meet their needs'
(ibid.: 9). Along similar lines, it is maintained that the expression 'needs' sig-
nals dependency, inadequacy and unworthiness (Corbett, 1996). Suggestions
for new terminology include the expression 'exceptional' children but it is
also intimated that such a term has limitations and is likely to be short lived
(Mittler, 2000: 10). An alternative view is that the term SEN can be more
clearly defined, and efforts are better placed in clarifying the definition and
seeking (at least local) agreement on its meaning rather than replacing the
term with short-lived substitutes (see Chapter 3).

Special education as progress

Although, as Corbett (1998: 12) points out, it is naïve to assume that the passage of time equates with 'inevitable progress', she indicates what do seem to
be clear indications of progress. Discussing the sentiments of the influential
psychologist, Cyril Burt, that to teach children in a special school with a
'mental ratio' of less that 50% is to squander time and energy, she observes
that these sentiments are 'shocking in their conservatism concerning cultural
horizons and appropriate limits' (ibid.: 10).

Special educational developments are sometimes seen as running beside
progress in scientific and other endeavours. One of the reasons why schools

for the handicapped were thought to lag behind schools for other children was that certain specialist techniques were necessary and were not developed in the early days of special education. Some of these awaited 'advances in science, medicine and mental measurement' (Pritchard, 1963: 1).

Blind people's status has been traced from their being objects of charity to being more independent. From the caricature of the blind beggar to the development of residential schools for the blind and methods of achieving literacy such as the Braille system, progress continued as the option of more local day schools became possible for blind children. The needs of children with sufficient vision potentially to read print became recognised as being different from those of children who would depend on touch. Technological advances, particularly the rendering of print and other visual information into sound, are taken to suggest that 'the history of blindness has entered a whole new era' (Safford and Safford, 1996: 152).

Inclusion relating to the education of increasing numbers of pupils with SEN in mainstream schools is an example of what many regard as progress, but historians of special education offer different views of inclusion or its precursors. Pritchard (1963) presented a picture of special education in which special schools and their development were the way forward. Tomlinson (1982) takes an essentially conflict view of the history of special education and questions the separation of children into special schools. Hurt (1988) maintains that educating children inside the mainstream is desirable, perhaps reflecting the fact that he was writing not long after the Warnock Report (DES, 1978) made recommendations that were expected to increase the number of children with SEN in mainstream schools. Cole (1989) offers a broader perspective than what he sees as the false dichotomy of the integration–segregation controversy, suggesting that the concept of integration informed many nineteenth-century pioneers.

Safford and Safford (1996) depict social goals in the nineteenth century as moving from curing the deviant to sheltering him or her from society to protecting society from him or her. Mental testing appeared to support the view that children with learning difficulties were ineducable. Safford and Safford regard progress as the shift away from such views and the move from the use of institutions to more community-based work.

More recently, through the SEN green paper *Excellence for All Children* (DfEE, 1997a), the *Programme for Action* (DfEE, 1998b), the Special Educational Needs and Disability Rights in Education Act 2001 and the *Special Educational Needs Code of Practice* (DfES, 2001a), the government has sought to set the direction for the future. Themes emerging from these developments include encouraging the inclusion of children in mainstream schools, given certain caveats (for a more detailed outline of special education legislation since the Warnock Report, see Farrell, 2002).

Regarding the history of special education and the issue of the balance of mainstream and special education, it has been said:

> If there is a clear lesson of history, it is that timeless questions such as whether one should take the special child to the expert, or the expert to the special child, or whether it is better to be normal in an abnormal special school or abnormal in an ordinary school, cannot be answered as dogmatically as many have wished (Cole, 1989: 175).

Suggestions about the issues that might be taken into account when political decisions are made about the future and role of local special schools are provided in Chapter 4.

Motives of educators

The possible motives of special educators are a source of debate. It has been suggested that in the early 1880s 'humanitarianism combined with Methodism and Evangelicalism to support schools for the blind and deaf' (Pritchard, 1963: 25). For individual educators, different motivations can be ascertained or inferred. From the 1760s, Thomas Braidwood used lip reading and writing to teach deaf children to speak and read. However, Braidwood is not always remembered favourably, in part because of his 'secretiveness' (ibid.: 15). In 1815 an American visitor found that teachers in deaf institutions in London, Birmingham and Edinburgh were all sworn to secrecy about their methods. Another reason for Bradwood's unfavourablity is nepotism – members of Braidwood's family were superintendents of three of the four institutions for the deaf.

Others are seen as more obviously compassionate. James Kerr, for example, was appointed as medical officer to the Bradford School Board in 1893, where he selected children to attend the first special classes for the mentally handicapped. Pritchard writes of him: 'where handicapped children were concerned, his outward harshness concealed a wealth of compassion' (ibid.: 129). Tomlinson (1982), however, is suspiscious of humanitarian or Christian reformist interpretations of developments and examines evidence indicating that vested interests and professional rivalry were also at work. Many examples can be given to support such a perspective. Laurent Clerc (1785–1869), who lost his hearing in infancy, viewed the secretiveness of pioneers in deaf education during the Enlightenment as a refusal to share their methods in the interests of the deaf community (cited in Lane, 1984). While such accounts are an unsettling alternative to more benevolent interpretations, a different perspective can, however, be taken. Seguin (1880) believed that the work of the early pioneers was an important contribution to integrating deaf people into a hearing society (Safford and Safford, 1996: 32). Cole, on the other hand, has doubts about what he pointedly calls 'some aspects of recent sociological interpretations of special education's history' (1989: 7). While he believes that there is some substance to the social control hypothesis, he also believes that humanitarian motives predominate: 'The moral belief and liberal humanitarianism of many contemporaries should not be underestimated in the late Victorian age, or for that matter in any period afterwards' (ibid.). An apparent example of this more benevolent interpretation is the work of Thomas Barnardo (founder of homes for destitute boys in England), who is reported to have looked after children in his own home (ibid.: 9). Contrary to the oft-quoted trends in hereditarian beliefs (which sometimes lead to eugenic views), other perspectives prevailed. Barnardo, for example, reportedly said that if children from slums could be removed from such conditions early enough, 'heredity counts for little' (Heywood, 1978).

Another view is that pioneers of education outside the mainstream 'were motivated by a desire for a more orderly society and a genuine concern for the socially, physically and mentally disadvantaged' but that this intermingled with considerations of social control (Hurt, 1988: 189).

Communication in the education of deaf children

Table 2.1 shows the number of schools and units in the UK for children who are deaf or who have hearing impairments and how those schools identified their approach to such children in the *National Deaf Children's Society Directory* of 1996.

In earlier times deaf people were often seen as 'deaf and dumb' but this was later replaced by an awareness among hearing people of what deafness really is, and of an awareness the relationship between speech and hearing, the distinctions between speech and language, and the integrity of signed communication (Safford and Safford, 1996).

Arguments for and against oralism and signing were expressed in the evidence taken in the hearings which led to the 1889 *Report of the Royal Commission on the Blind, the Deaf and Others of the United Kingdom*. Supporters of a combined system took the view that it gave the deaf the advantages of

Table 2.1 National Deaf Children's Society Directory *(1996) schools and units for children who are deaf or have hearing impairments*

	Total communication	Oral	Bilingualism	Declined to specify
No. of schools	15	7	4	5
No. of units	104	129	15	220

both signing and oralism. However, the commissioners felt that, all too often, the manual alphabet prevailed and so pupils were denied the use of speech (Pritchard, 1963: 102). Approaches that have emphasised oralism or signing have led to different versions of history, as indicated by such books as *The Conquest of Deafness* (Bender, 1970) and *When the Mind Hears* (Lane, 1984), the titles of which indicate their position. More modern debates about the effectiveness of different methods identify oral approaches, total communication and sign bilingualism.

Oral approaches, (that recognise that most children who are deaf or have hearing impairments are born to hearing parents) aim to teach these children to speak (so that they can communicate with their own family and others who can hear) and to understand spoken language. It is assumed that these children will then be able to use their spoken language as a language for thought and as a foundation for literacy skills, thus gaining access to the wider curriculum (Watson, 1998). Having grasped spoken language, deaf people can choose whether to continue to use spoken language exclusively or to learn deaf sign language (e.g. British Sign Language). It is not considered feasible first to learn deaf sign language then spoken language because the best way to develop spoken language is to use residual hearing from as early an age as possible. Cochlear implants are considered necessary from an early age for similar reasons. The early use of aids to hearing is also important. Deaf Education through Listening and Talking (DELTA) support an oral approach (sometimes called 'natural oralism'), which has some similarities to, but also some differences from, the maternal reflective approach (Andrews, 1988).

Concerning oral approaches generally, as Watson (1998: 73) points out, it is unhelpful to have too narrow a focus on exploiting hearing 'without placing it in the wider context of communication'. This could disrupt the normal pattern of interaction between baby and parent, which leads to the development of early communication and, later, spoken language.

Regarding total communication (TC), the use of signing and talking has precursors in the work of the Abbé de l'Epée in France who, in 1765, began teaching two deaf sisters and invented a sign language to assist in this. Denton, then Superintendent of the Maryland School for the Deaf, defined TC as including 'the full spectrum of language modes, child-devised gestures, the language of signs, speech, speech reading, finger spelling, reading and writing' (1976: 4). However, to be effective, TC requires fluency in signing on the part of parents and early educators. Many schools and units in the UK that describe their approach as TC (Baker and Knight, 1998) support a definition developed by the Leeds Local Education Authority Deaf and Hearing Impaired Support Service (Leeds Local Education Authority, 1995), which has an underpinning philosophy, bases the choice of method on individual pupil's needs and identifies specific language use (see Case Study 2.1).

Case Study 2.1 *Total communication at Doncaster School for the Deaf*

Doncaster School for the Deaf (founded in 1829) is an independent special school for resident and day pupils from nursery age to 16 years. It shares a campus with the Doncaster College for the Deaf which offers post-16 education and training. The approach to language and communication uses 'graphic communication' based on the maternal reflective method developed in the Netherlands by van Uden (1977). It encourages the use of natural language, enabling the child to acquire and use English naturally. Drawing on developmental principles, this involves conversational exchanges between the deaf child and a more mature language user. The conversation is used to analyse and discuss grammatical structure. Writing is used to support spoken language.

The school has a TC policy that promotes the development of speech and natural language, preparing pupils for effective communication, with deaf and hearing people. TC is seen as the use of any mode of communication, including speech and one of the forms of manual communication – finger spelling, gestures, facial expression, body language, lip reading and amplification.

Source: Information kindly supplied by the Doncaster School for the Deaf.

Sign bilingualism uses both the sign language of the deaf community and the spoken and written languages of the hearing community. The balance of languages varies depending on individual requirements (Baker, 1993).

Milestones in the history of special education in England

The eighteenth century

1760 Thomas Braidwood tutors a deaf child using an oral method which leads to the development of his Academy for the Deaf and Dumb in Edinburgh and the beginning of a Braidwood family dynasty in the education of the deaf in Britain lasting until 1878.

1765 Opening of the Asylum for the Industrious Blind, Edinburgh, and the Asylum for the Blind in Clifton, Bristol.

1765 In France, Abbé de l'Epée begins teaching two deaf sisters, later inventing a sign language to assist.

1791 Henry Dannett founds the School for the Instruction of the Indigent Blind in Liverpool (indigent = poor and needy).

1792 The Asylum for the Support and Education of the Deaf and Dumb Children of the Poor opens in Bermondsey, London, with Joseph Watson, the second nephew of Thomas Braidwood, in charge.

The nineteenth century

1800 The School for the Indigent Blind, London, opens, aimed at instructing the blind in a trade.

1805 Thomas Tawell opens the Asylum and School for the Indigent Blind in Norwich, catering for children and elderly blind people.

1806 Joseph Watson publishes *Instruction of the Deaf and Dumb* following the death of Thomas Braidwood, setting out Watson's oral approach supplemented by manual methods, which had previously been kept secret.

1812 The General Institution for the Instruction of Deaf and Dumb Children is established in Birmingham with Thomas Braidwood, grandson of the first Thomas Braidwood, as principal.

1819 John Arrowsmith publishes *The Art of Instructing the Infant Deaf and Dumb*, advocating the early education of deaf children.

1829 Louis Braille introduces his system of embossed dots which he teaches at the Institution Nationale des Jeunes Aveugles, Paris, although it would be 1872 before the first English school teaches Braille.

1835 The Yorkshire School for the Deaf and Blind opens in York and begins using books with embossed types for the blind as well as concentrating on industrial training.

1837 Seguin begins his first educational work with 'idiots' and the 'feeble-minded' in the hospices of Paris, involving the systematic training of the senses.

1838 The London Society for Teaching the Blind to Read is established.

1839 The Blind Asylum opens in Manchester.

1841 The Catholic Blind Asylum opens in Liverpool under the Sisters of Charity of St Vincent de Paul, the first school in England for handicapped children to be established by a religious body.

1847 The Royal Cambrian Institution for the Deaf and Dumb, the first school for handicapped children in Wales, opens in Aberystwyth.

1847 William Moon devises his embossed type using Roman letters, with some modifications.

1847 The Asylum for Idiots opens in Highgate, London.

1851 The Cripples Home and Industrial School for Girls in founded in Marylebone.

1859 The Eastern Counties Asylum (for idiots) opens in Colchester.

1860 The first infants' school for handicapped (deaf) children opens in Manchester.

1862 Susannah Hull opens a private school, teaching deaf children by the oral method.

1865 The National Industrial Home and School for Crippled Boys opens in Kensington.

1866 The College for the Blind Sons of Gentlemen opens in Worcester, emphasising classics, divinity, English literature and mathematics.

1869 The Charity Organisation Society is formed to encourage new charitable efforts and to co-ordinate existing ones.

1870 Forster's Education Act gives powers to form school boards to provide elementary education for all children.

1871 The Association for the Oral Instruction of the Deaf and Dumb is established.

1872 The London School Board is formed, and its provision for deaf children is the first time that such education is assisted by public funds.

1872 The Royal Normal College opens at Norwood to provide a liberal and musical education for the blind, teaching in Braille.

1873 The London Home Teaching Society arranges for some of its teachers to visit National Schools in London to teach the Moon system to any blind child admitted.

1876 A report of the Charity Organisation Society's special committee on the education of the blind advocates that the blind should be educated with sighted children in public elementary schools.

1878 The Darenth School for Imbeciles (for children) and the Darenth Asylum (for those over 16 years old) opens.

1880 In the 1880s, centres for educating blind children open, all attached to ordinary schools, and blind pupils spend half their time or more being educated with sighted children.

1886 The Idiots Act is passed, permitting existing institutions to admit mentally defective children at their parents' wish.

1888 The Invalid Children's Aid Association is founded.

1889 Publication of the *Report of the Royal Commission on the Blind, the Deaf and Dumb and Others of the United Kingdom* (the Egerton Commission). Recommendations for the blind included that there should be compulsory education from 5 to 16 years provided by school authorities. Recommendations for the deaf included that no one system of teaching should be endorsed and that compulsory education should be from 7 to 16 years. Recommendations were also made for the idiots, imbeciles and the feeble-minded. Most imbeciles would require residential training but their teachers should be drawn from ordinary schools and their education should continue where necessary to the age of 21 years. Feeble-minded children should be taught in auxiliary schools, with special provision.

1890 Following the *Report of the Royal Commission* of 1889, the Education of Blind and Deaf Mute Children (Scotland) Act is passed.

1892 The Leicester School Board sets up the first school of special instruction (for feeble-minded children).

1892 Three months after the Leicester special school opens, the London School Board opens its first school of special instruction, the Hugh Myddleton School.

1893 Margaret McMillan and James Kerr (medical officer) are appointed to the Bradford School Board.

1893 Following the *Report of the Royal Commission* of 1889, the Elementary (Blind and Deaf Children) Act is passed. School authorities are placed under a duty to enable blind children and deaf children to receive efficient and suitable provision in a school established (or contributed to) by the school authority if such an education was otherwise unobtainable. Blind children are to be educated from 5 to 16 years; deaf children from 7 to 16 years.

1894 The Women's University Settlement at Southwark opens a class for physically handicapped children in a room in the London School Board's centre for deaf children.

1898 The *Report of the Committee on Defective and Epileptic Children* is published.

1899 Following the *Report of the Committee on Defective and Epileptic Children* of 1898, the Elementary Education (Defective and Epileptic Children) Act is passed permitting school authorities to provide for the education of mentally and physically defective and epileptic children.

1899 The Passmore Edwards Settlement School, London, the first school for physically handicapped pupils, opens.

The twentieth century to the present

1900 The Union of Women Workers establishes of the Victoria Street Settlement in Liverpool and the Cripples' School in 1897, leading to the opening of the school for physically handicapped pupils at Shaw Street, Liverpool – the second school for physically handicapped pupils in England.

1901 The first hospital school is established at the West Kirby Convalescent Home for Children, Liverpool.

1901 A convalescent home for children is established by Agnes Hunt, which later becomes the Shropshire Surgical Home – the world's first open-air hospital for cripples.

1902 A residential school for feeble-mined children opens at Sandlebridge, Cheshire.

1903 The school for the Roman Catholic colony for epileptics, at Much Hadham, Hertfordshire, is approved by the Board of Education.

1905 Manchester LEA establishes the Swinton House School for the recovery of physically handicapped children.

1907 The College of Teachers for the Blind is established, awarding qualifications recognised by the Board of Education.

1908 The Lord Mayor Treloar Cripples Hospital and College opens in Alton, Hampshire

1908 The world's first special class for highly myopic and other children with defective vision is opened by the London County Council in Camberwell.

1909 A joint examining board diploma for teachers of the deaf is recognised by the Ministry of Education.

1913 The Mental Deficiency Act is passed. Education authorities are placed under a duty to ascertain which children aged 7 to 16 are defective and then to decide which of these are incapable of being educated in a special school. These children they would pass to the mental deficiency committee.

1914 The Elementary Education (Defective and Epileptic Children) Act is passed, having the effect of making the 1899 Act obligatory, not permissive, in relation to mentally defective children.

1918 The National Institute for the Blind opens its first Sunshine Home at Chorly Wood, Hertfordshire, for blind children aged 2 to 5.

1921 Chorley Wood College opens for the higher education of blind girls.

1929 The *Report of the Mental Deficiency Committee* (the Wood Committee) is published.

1934 The Cripples Training College, Leatherhead (later the Queen Elizabeth's Training College for the Disabled), opens.

1934 Publication of the *Report of the Committee of Enquiry into Problems Relating to Partially Sighted Children.*

1938 Publication of the *Report of the Committee of Inquiry into the Problems Relating to Children with Defective Hearing.*

1944 The Butler Education Act requires education authorities to have regard to the need 'for securing that provision is made for pupils who suffer from any disability of mind or body by providing, either in special schools, or otherwise, special educational treatment' (7 and 8 George VI Chapter 31 section 8). Certification by the medical officer, which previously determined whether a child should attend special school, ends, and LEAs now make this decision.

1945 The *Handicapped Pupils and School Health Service Regulations* are published. The previously recognised five handicaps (blind, deaf, epileptic, physically defective, mentally defective) are extended to eleven (blind, partially sighted, deaf, partially deaf, epileptic, physically handicapped, delicate, diabetic, educationally subnormal, speech defect, maladjusted).

1945 The College of Speech Therapists is founded as an organising and examinations body.

1955 *The Report of the Committee on Maladjusted Children* is published.

1970 The Education (Handicapped Children) Act is passed under which the notion of ineducabilty associated with 'severely subnormal' children in the Education Act 1944 is removed and the education of all children becomes the responsibility of the LEA.

1978 Publication of *Special Educational Needs: Report of the Committee of Inquiry into the Education of Handicapped Children and Young People* (the Warnock report). The term 'special education' should be broadened and most special education should take place in schools. The concept of 'special educational need' should replace that of categories of handicap.

1981 Following the Warnock Report, the Education Act 1981 provides a new legal definition of 'special educational need'. The definition continues to be used in subsequent education Acts and is currently the legal definition in the Education Act 1996. The 1981 Act also provided for the statutory assessment of SEN and for statement of SEN by LEAs.

1989 The Children Act 1989 sets out the responsibilities of a local authority towards a child. It also sets out the legal definition of parental responsibility.

1993 The Education Act 1993 seeks to introduce improved provision for children with SEN, building on the Education Act 1981. It provides for the formation of a SEN Tribunal to hear cases where LEAs and parents disagree about the assessment of SEN and other matters.

1994 The *Code of Practice on the Identification and Assessment of Special Educational Needs* is published, giving guidance on procedures for the graduated identification and assessment of pupils with SEN.

1995 The Disability Discrimination Act requires each county, voluntary and grant-maintained school to publish new information relating to disability in their annual reports.

1997 The consultation paper *Excellence for All Children: Meeting Special Educational Needs* is published, which seeks to encourage the inclusion of more pupils with SEN in mainstream schools.

1998 *Meeting Special Educational Needs: A Programme for Action* is published, setting out proposed action relating to issues raised in the 1997 consultation paper.

2001 The Special Educational Needs and Disability Act is passed, strengthening the right of children with SEN to be educated in mainstream schools under specified conditions. The remit of the SEN Tribunal is extended to include appeals against disability discrimination in education and the tribunal becomes the SEN and Disability Tribunal (SENDIST).

2001 The *Special Educational Needs Code of Practice* is published, building on the guidance of the 1994 code.

Thinking points

Practitioners may wish to consider, from a historical perspective:

- the benefits and limitations of the term 'special educational needs'; and
- to what extent the motives of special educators can be criticised as reflecting vested interests, and to what degree they may be considered humanitarian.

Key texts

Farrell, M. (2002) *The Special Education Handbook* (3rd edn). London: David Fulton.
    This book includes appendices summarising SEN legislation, reports and consultative
    documents, regulations and guidance from the time of the Warnock Report to the present.
Safford, P.L. and Safford, E.J. (1996) *A History of Childhood and Disability* New York, NY: Teachers
    College Press.
    While the remit of this book is not quite as wide as it may appear at first, it provides a broad
    historical view of attitudes to, and provision for, children with learning difficulties and
    disabilities.

3

Legal Definitions of SEN, Local Criteria and SENDIST

Introduction

This chapter sets out the definition of SEN as contained in the Education Act 1996. Several legal definitions of disability are then considered. Returning to the Education Act 1996, the chapter looks at the expression 'difficulty in learning' and its possible relationships with pupil progress and standards of achievement, and at the term 'disability' and its relationship to facilities/resources. SEN is considered in terms of 'learning difficulty', 'difficulty in learning' and 'disability'. The chapter examines relationships between the continuum of SEN and the continuum of support. It considers local criteria for SEN and locally allocated funding and support for SEN. The work of the Special Educational Needs and Disability Tribunal (SENDIST) is outlined. A tension is identified between judgements made by the tribunal seeing each child as an individual and the broader approach to LEA funding related more widely to levels of learning difficulties and the disabilities of children.

The legal definition of SEN

The definition of SEN contained in the Education Act 1996 is as follows: 'a child has special educational needs . . . if he has a learning difficulty which calls for special educational provision to be made for him' (s. 312). In defining 'learning difficulty', the Act states that a child has a learning difficulty if:

a) he has a significantly greater difficulty in learning than the majority of children of his age;

b) he has a disability which either prevents or hinders him from making use of educational facilities of a kind generally provided for children of his age in schools within the area of the local education authority; or

c) he is under the age of five and is, or would be if special educational provision were not made for him, likely to fall within paragraph (a) and (b) when of, or over that age (s. 312 (2)).

Legal definitions of disability

As well as the perspective on disability within the definition of SEN in the Education Act 1996, there are different definitions elsewhere in legislation. The Children Act (England and Wales) 1989 describes children with disabilities within a wider context of children 'in need', which allows eligibility for certain support and services from the local authority. Under s. 17 of the Act a child is 'in need' if:

(a) he/she is unlikely to achieve or maintain, or to have the opportunity of achieving or maintaining a reasonable standard of health or development without the provisions for him/her of services by a local authority under this [part] of the Act;
(b) his/her health or development is likely to be significantly impaired, or further impaired, without the provision for him/her of such services or;
(c) he/she is disabled.

'Development' refers to physical, intellectual, emotional, social or behavioural development while 'health' encompasses physical and mental health. The Act states that: 'A child is disabled if he is blind, deaf or dumb or suffers from mental disorder of any kind or is substantially and permanently handicapped by illness, injury or congenital deformity or other such disability as may be prescribed.'

The Disability Discrimination Act 1995 defines a disabled person as someone who has: 'a physical or mental impairment which has a substantial and long term adverse effect on his ability to carry out normal day-to-day activities.' The term 'physical or mental impairments' includes sensory impairments (such as those affecting sight or hearing), learning difficulties and clinically recognised mental illness. The Special Educational Needs and Disability Rights in Education Act 2001 amended the Disability Discrimination Act 1995 to cover every aspect of education. It inserted a new Part 4 to prevent discrimination against disabled people in their access to education.

Chapter 1 of the new Part 4 sets out the requirements for those who provide school education, in which there are duties making it unlawful to discriminate, without justification, against disabled pupils in all aspects of school life. The Act indicates that not all disabled children will have an SEN or a learning difficulty, although many will. A *Disability Code of Practice*

(Schools) (Disability Rights Commission, 2001a) provides guidance to schools and LEAs in England and Wales.

'Difficulty in learning' and pupil progress and achievement

The Education Act 1996 refers to difficulty in learning 'significantly greater' than that of children 'of his age', but the word 'significantly' is open to interpretation. One way of seeking to identify such a level of difficulty in learning is to relate it to evidence of pupils making slow progress and, as a result, of reaching lower standards of achievement than the majority of children. From this perspective, regarding, for example, a difficulty such as 'profound and multiple learning difficulty', a pupil's progress is considered to be very slow and standards of achievement considerably lower than that of children who do not have such difficulties. Personal and social development standards are also important (Farrell, 2001: 3–12).

Disability and resources

'Disability' in the Education Act 1996

When considering SEN, the most appropriate definition of disability is contained in the Education Act 1996. That Act, as noted earlier, concerns disability that hinders or prevents a child from making use of educational facilities of a kind generally provided for children of his or her age in schools within the area of the local education authority.

The relationship between disability and facilities/resources

This definition implies that, in a specified LEA, a child's disability will be seen in the context of the 'educational facilities' that are 'of a kind' generally provided in schools in the LEA's area. If schools in one area generally provide to a greater degree for a certain disability than another LEA, this will reflect back on the disability so that it might constitute a learning difficulty. This means that LEAs therefore need to specify the type of disability and the degree of disability for which schools in their areas cannot generally provide.

One way of clarifying the educational implications of a disability is through thresholds or criteria to determine the degree of disability at which extra funding or other support is agreed. For example, an LEA may specify the degree of hearing loss that constitutes hearing impairment so as to warrant the involvement of a qualified teacher of the deaf (see Case Study 3.2) or the initiation of a statutory assessment of SEN. This does not, however, indicate how the child should learn, which suggests that such approaches are not over-rigid.

Where LEAs delegate funding and other resources (such as equipment) to their schools to differing degrees, it is more difficult for several LEAs to agree a common point at which the statutory assessment of SEN would be considered. This is because one LEA may claim that the resources it has delegated to a school should provide a similar level of support for a pupil with SEN that, in another LEA, would require statutory assessment and the extra funding normally associated with a statement of SEN.

This does not diminish, however, the importance of having a clear definition of the form and level of disability in a particular LEA that, with regard to a particular child: 'either prevents or hinders him from making use of educational facilities of a kind generally provided for children of his age in schools within the area of the local education authority' (s. 312 Education Act 1996). Where this differs from LEA to LEA, it may be difficult to convey the reason for this to parents. If a parent of a child with a disability moves from one LEA area to another, it could be that his or her former LEA agreed to a statutory assessment while the 'new' LEA refuses one for the same child. Unless the second LEA can demonstrate clearly the differences in the level of funding between itself and the first LEA, it will be difficult to account for the apparent anomaly with any credibility.

The more groups of LEAs can agree similar levels of delegation and, therefore, have similar expectations of their schools regarding the point at which a statutory assessment is fitting, the greater will be the perceived level of consistency. Where LEAs are adjacent, such agreement will be encouraged if LEA officers and others meet to discuss their respective arrangements for funding and the possibilities of longer-term agreed levels of delegation.

SEN and 'learning difficulty' in relation to 'difficulty in learning' and 'disability'

As noted above, there are layers in the definition of SEN. A pupil does *not* have a 'learning difficulty' (still less an SEN) if he or she has a difficulty in learning that is not 'significantly greater' than children of the same age. Nor does a child have a learning difficulty if he or she has a disability that does not 'either prevent or hinder him from making use of educational facilities' as described in the Education Act 1996. Only if the pupil has a 'difficulty in learning' or a 'disability' as indicated by the Act is he or she considered to have a 'learning difficulty'. And only if the pupil has a learning difficulty that 'calls for special educational provision' to be made does the child have 'special educational needs'.

This definition of SEN, therefore, has two variables. The first is the meaning attached to the word 'significantly' in the 'learning difficulty' layer of the definition. The second relates to what educational facilities are 'generally provided'.

SEN and triggers for support

The *Special Educational Needs Code of Practice* (DfES, 2001a) indicates a graduated approach to SEN. Its glossary defines a graduated approach (ibid.: 203) as:

> a model of action and intervention in schools and early education settings to help children who have special educational needs. The approach recognises that there is a continuum of special educational needs and that, where necessary, increasing specialist expertise should be brought to bear on the difficulties that the child may be experiencing.

Given that there is considered to be a continuum of SEN and 'increasing specialist expertise', it seems sensible to relate the two so that lower and higher levels of difficulty are related, respectively, to lower and higher levels of support.

A threshold document originally appended to the *Special Educational Needs Draft Code of Practice* (DfEE, 2000h) was not appended to the final *Special Educational Needs Code of Practice* (DfEE, 2001a). The draft document went some way to indicate the sort of levels of SEN that might be associated with triggers for different forms of support. It aimed to give those involved in responding to pupils' SEN a framework to help them decide 'appropriate forms of action to meet particular patterns and levels of special educational needs and review their decisions' (DfEE, 2000h: 3). The forms of action/support (as set out in the final version of the code), include the following:

■ 'School action', in which a class/subject teacher provides interventions that are additional to or different from those provided as part of the school's usual differentiated curriculum and strategies.
■ 'school action plus', in which the class/subject teacher and the SEN co-ordinator are given advice or support from outside specialists to enable interventions to be put in place that are additional to or different from those provided for pupils through 'school action'.
■ Statements of SEN, perhaps involving such provision as 'regular and frequent direct teaching by a specialist teacher; daily individual support from a learning support assistant; a significant piece of equipment such as a closed circuit television or a computer or CD-ROM device with appropriate ancillaries and software; the regular involvement of non-educational agencies' (DfES, 2001a: s. 8.13).

Regarding 'general learning difficulties', the threshold document (DfEE, 2000h: 13) indicated that lower levels of difficulty might be indicated by such factors as: 'performance within the National Curriculum below the level within which most children are expected to work (i.e. level 1 at the end of KS1; level 2/3 at KS2; level 3/4 at KS3) Higher levels of difficulty might be indicated by such factors as: 'performance within the National Curriculum below the level within which most children are expected to work (i.e. level W at the end of KS1; level 1 at KS2; level 2 at KS3)' (ibid.).

The threshold document gives case studies with commentaries indicating how pupils' levels of difficulty and their progress might be considered in relation to different levels of support. Similarly, an attempt is made to relate different levels of disability (such as blindness) to an appropriate response. Lower levels of difficulty may be indicated by such features as 'problems in undertaking tasks or participating in those activities dependent on vision' and by an impact on progress and standards. Higher levels of difficulty are indicated by such things as 'inability to make progress in the curriculum without the use of specialist materials and equipment' (ibid.: 43)

Local agreement on criteria

Successive governments have not provided criteria relating to what level of 'difficulty in learning' makes a 'significantly greater' one that would contribute to learning difficulty and that could lead to the child having SEN. Neither has there been national guidance on disability in relation to SEN as this is particularly difficult where disability is defined in terms of what is generally provided at a local level. Therefore it is the LEAs themselves who try to define those degrees of difficulty in learning and disability that are likely to be considered learning difficulties and that may require special educational provision.

This is complicated by the fact that a significant difficulty in learning and disability may occur in the same child (for example, a pupil with severe learning difficulty may also have a disability such as blindness). But determining what constitutes SEN implies the participants agreeing the necessary criteria so that decisions about which children are considered to have SEN and which children are not are less arbitrary than would be otherwise be the case. Local authorities, schools, parents and others try to ensure they are clear about what SEN is taken to mean, and many LEAs have made considerable efforts in this direction.

An LEA may set criteria for considering statutory assessment in terms of evidence from the school of strategies that have already been employed. For example, in relation to emotional and behavioural difficulties, an LEA may require evidence of strategies that have already been adopted to modify the pupil's behaviour both in school and at home. It may also require that the difficulties have been present for some time and have occurred in different settings. Criteria are also set out in relation to standardised assessments, as Case Study 3.1 illustrates.

Case Study 3.1 *Croydon LEA criteria for initiating a statutory assessment of SEN*

Since 1997, Croydon LEA has used well established criteria for initiating statutory assessment. These are being further developed to link with early years action/plus and school action/plus. Criteria for different SEN have been developed for moderate learning difficulties; specific learning difficulties; emotional and behavioural difficulties; physical disability; hearing difficulties; visual difficulties; speech, language and communication difficulties; and autism. Some examples are given below.

Moderate learning difficulties

For children below the age of 7, attainments would be at (or lower than) the level of an average child two and a half years younger in two or more of the areas of communication skills, concept development, early literacy, early numeracy skills, self-help skills and mobility skills.

For children at Key Stage 2 and above there should be evidence that a child's attainments in *either* reading or number on appropriate standardised tests are at or below the first centile (that is, the lowest-scoring 1% of the pupil population); or a child's attainments in *both* reading and number on appropriate tests are at or below the second centile (that is, the lowest-scoring 2% of the pupil population).

Specific learning difficulties (e.g. dyslexia)

The most significant factor for pupils with specific learning difficulties is a child's reading, spelling or writing difficulty rather than his or her intelligence quotient score.

For a child to be considered for statutory assessment relating to dyslexia, the literacy levels have to be significantly below age-average, as follows:

Age (chronological)	Literacy level*
7/8	no significant attainment in reading, writing or number
8	5 years 8 months
9	6 years
10	6 years 3 months
11	6 years 6 months
12	7 years
13	7 years 4 months
14	7 years 6 months

* Children functioning below this level who have had intervention would be considered to have a significant difficulty.

Physical disability

The LEA considers statutory assessment if there is clear evidence that the pupil's physical and mobility difficulties are limiting access to the full National Curriculum, despite all the efforts being made by the school.

Speech, language and communication difficulties

In most cases, statutory assessment will be required for children who:

- cannot communicate without help from another person or a technological device;
- communicate verbally but with the help of a signing (non-verbal) system;
- cannot communicate effectively because they cannot see things from another person's point of view so that their language is totally egocentric, and where the difficulty impedes learning to the degree that they cannot follow the National Curriculum; or
- have a disorder of speech and language such that intensive speech and language therapy needs to be a part of their educational programme.

Source: Information kindly supplied by Croydon LEA.

The implications of the Croydon criteria for moderate learning difficulties are that pupils considered to have severe learning difficulties would score on a lower percentile than pupils with moderate learning difficulties. Pupils considered as having profound and multiple learning difficulties would be expected to score on a lower percentile than pupils with severe learning difficulties.

LEA criteria are also used to gain access to specialist provision to help ensure this is appropriately allocated, as Case Study 3.2 indicates.

Case study 3.2 *Northamptonshire LEA criteria for the involvement of qualified teachers of the deaf/visually impaired*

For the involvement of a qualified teacher of the visually impaired, the LEA requires that the child:

- has a visual acuity of 6/18 or less;
- is a Braille or adapted print user;
- has a deteriorating visual condition;
- has a significantly reducing field of vision; or
- has visual perceptual difficulties.

For the involvement of a qualified teacher of the deaf, the LEA requires that the average hearing loss in the 'better' ear should be 40 decibels or greater; or the loss would normally be sensory-neural although, in a few cases, it could be a long-standing conductive loss.

Source: Information kindly supplied by Northamptonshire LEA.

Local funding and support for SEN

SEN is defined and identified to determine which pupils will receive special provision and which will not. This preferential provision (usually associated with higher-than-normal levels of pupil funding) is justified by the circumstances of individual pupils. If there is no broad local agreement, this may lead to competition for a greater proportion of resources, the result being inequitable funding. Even where good practice involves clusters of schools agreeing how they are to distribute funds, local agreement is useful in relation to how these funds may be allocated fairly. Similarly, where there has been progress in developing regional partnerships for SEN, how the support is to be allocated must be agreed according to some form of established criteria. It could be argued that such a view of funding and support assumes some absolute state of learning difficulty or disability. It could be further maintained that it is important to respond to the challenge of differentiation, ensuring that pupils are provided with appropriate levels of work and support. But if differentiation is not to be random, it must to be based on something. In other words, when one uses expressions such as 'appropriate levels of support', one needs some indication of what 'appropriate' means in this context.

Similarly, when LEAs seek to agree criteria for SEN and related broad bands of funding, this allows schools to fine tune the support they need through teachers' and others professional judgement. It also enables schools to adjust the funding they receive for a particular pupil through the use of some of the money they receive through formula funding. No rigid understandings of SEN are therefore implied, and nor is a rigid approach to support and funding. All that is sought is a broad and equitable approach to funding at the local level which tries to prevent the larger part of the funding going to the strongest lobby rather than to pupils with the greatest degree of disabilty and the most significant difficulty in learning.

The Special Educational Needs and Disability Tribunal (SENDIST)

The Special Educational Needs and Disability Tribunal (SENDIST) seeks to resolve disputes between parents and an LEA. SENDIST is an independent tribunal set up by an Act of Parliament of 1993, originally as the SEN Tribunal. Its remit was widened in 2001 to take account of the requirements of the Special Educational Needs and Disability Rights in Education Act 2001. The tribunal considers parents' appeals against the decisions of LEAs about a child's SEN when the parents and the LEA cannot agree.

SENDIST strives to be easily accessible and to resolve disputes fairly and quickly. Parents may present their case in person or can bring a friend or relative to speak for them if they prefer. Hearings take place within reasonable travelling distance of the parents' home (for example, most appeals in London and the south-east are heard at the tribunal's London headquarters).

Each appeal is heard by three tribunal members: a legally qualified chairperson, and two lay members with experience in special educational needs and/or in local government. The chair gives a decision (binding on both parties to the appeal) in writing and explains the reasons behind it. Tribunal decisions are final. The tribunal has jurisdiction over LEAs but not over individual schools.

Parents can appeal to SENDIST if the LEA refuses to:

- carry out a formal assessment of SEN on their child; or
- issue a statement of the child's SEN.

If the LEA has made a statement, or if it has changed an earlier statement, parents may appeal against:

- the parts of the statement describing the child's SEN (part 2);
- the parts which set out the special educational help the LEA considers the child should receive (part 3);
- the school named in the statement (part 4); or
- the LEA not naming a school.

Parents may appeal if the LEA:

- refuses to change the school named in the child's statement where the statement is at least a year old;
- refuses to reassess the child's SEN if the LEA has not made a new assessment for at least six months;
- decides not to maintain the child's statement;
- decides not to change the statement; or
- parents may appeal to the SENDIST if they consider that their child has been discriminated against unfairly by a *school* because of the child's disability.

Timescales are laid down for the appeal process.

SENDIST, like the SEN Tribunal before it, comes to its decisions 'by considering all the evidence' (Special Educational Needs Tribunal, 2001: 28). Both parents and LEAs can appeal to the High Court against SENDIST decisions.

Every year since the SEN Tribunal was formed (and more recently since it evolved into SENDIST) there has been an increase in appeals registered so that, by the year 2001–2, it registered 3,048 appeals. This compares with

Table 3.1 *Grounds for the majority of appeals (2001–2)*

Grounds	%
Refusal to assess	37.4
The contents of a statement (parts 2, 3 and 4)	24.0
The contents of the statement (parts 2 and 3)	13.3
The contents of the statement (part 4)	11.2
Refusal to make a statement	8.0

Source: Special Educational Needs and Disability Tribunal (2002: 7).

1,161 appeals registered in 1994–5 (Special Educational Needs and Disability Tribunal, 2002: 5–6). Table 3.1 indicates the grounds for most of the appeals in the year 2001–2. The remaining appeals were against refusal to *re*-assess, refusal to change the name of the school, a decision to cease making a statement and failure to name a school. Table 3.2 shows the main types of SEN of pupils registered in the year 2000–1.

Some 75% of appeals were related to the areas shown in Table 3.2 while the rest concerned physical disabilities, moderate learning difficulties, severe learning difficulties, hearing impairment, epilepsy, visual impairment, multi-sensory impairment and 'other/unknown' SEN.

The outcomes of appeals indicate that they are usually successful from the point of view of parents, with 76% of appeals succeeding in the year 2001–2. In all types of appeal (except those against 'refusal to reassess' and 'refusal to statement'), the percentage of appeals upheld was 67% or above. In one area (appeals against the contents of a statement parts 2, 3 and 4) it was 93%.

Table 3.2 *Main types of SEN of pupils whose cases were registered with SENDIST in the year 2000–1*

Type of SEN	%
Literacy (including specific learning difficulties)	34.5
Autism	16.1
Emotional and behavioural difficulties	14.2
Speech and language difficulties	10.2

Source: Special Educational Needs and Disability Tribunal (2002: 8).

■ SENDIST's work

The approach to individual cases

The annual report of 1999–2000 (Special Educational Needs Tribunal, 2000) rejected the possibility of a uniform approach to SEN because SENDIST looks at individual cases and emphasises the fact that no two cases are the same. The annual report stated that:

> The difficulties, disabilities, experiences and circumstances of the children whose educational needs we consider vary almost infinitely. Direct comparisons between two apparently similar cases are nearly always misleading . . . Some might consider it desirable to be able to say that a certain level of support would always be appropriate for a child with certain test results. But it is clear from the representations made to the Tribunal and from the views of the experienced Tribunal members, that such a mechanistic approach does not commend itself to educationalists. I therefore reject any suggestion that the Tribunal should act consistently in that sense (ibid.: 16).

A difficulty with this approach is that, if it is accepted that 'The difficulties, disabilities, experiences and circumstances of the children whose educational needs we consider vary almost infinitely', there can be no criteria on which to make judgements about what is appropriate in each case. If this were so there would be no point in distinguishing between different areas of SEN, such as profound and multiple learning difficulties or emotional and behavioural difficulties (EBD). It would make no sense to say that a child had EBD because this would not indicate that he shared anything in common with any other children who were identified as having EBD, because such children's educational needs 'vary almost infinitely'.

However, such distinctions are made. For example, advocate groups for children with a particular condition (such as autism) and their parents believe they are representing concerns relating to a condition with common features. The *Special Educational Needs Code of Practice* (DfEE, 2001a) considers different areas of SEN, such as moderate, severe and profound learning difficulties (ibid.: 7.58). Also, the tribunal's own reports show findings relating to what it calls 'types of disability'. These are autism, EBD, epilepsy, hearing impairment, literacy (including specific learning difficulty), moderate learning difficulty, multi-sensory impairments, physical disabilities, severe learning difficulties and visual impairment (Special Educational Needs and Disability Tribunal, 2002: 8, 10).

This does not suggest that a child's learning difficulties or disabilities are always best described by reference to one 'area' of SEN, such as 'emotional and behaviour difficulty' or 'speech and language difficulty'. Sometimes a child has SEN that relates to several 'areas'. However, when LEAs consider broad funding issues and the cost of support for individual pupils, they often assume there are broad differences. For example, a child with profound learning difficulties is assumed to require more support and funding than a child with moderate learning difficulties. In the LEA context, assumptions are made about children collectively, including the level of support likely to be suitable.

The SENDIST annual report quoted above states that 'Some might consider it desirable to be able to say that a certain level of support would always be appropriate for a child with certain test results'. The tribunal rejects such a view. However, from the LEA's point of view, consistency may be greater if a certain level of support were accepted as normally appropriate for a child assessed in an agreed way. For example, children who are behind in reading at a certain level may be considered as having SEN. If such criteria are not applied it is open for schools and parents to invent their own idiosyncratic understandings of SEN because the learning needs of children vary 'almost infinitely'.

The tribunal's view that, in this context, the learning needs of children may vary 'almost infinitely' is clearly at odds with broad LEA approaches to funding. Many LEAs are seeking to allocate support and funding consistently and according to some transparent system that is related to authority-wide criteria agreed through consultation. Such an approach allows the fine tuning of funding and support schools receive from other sources in relation to SEN generally. Where this does not complement individually based SENDIST decisions, and where these decisions relate to funding, SENDIST decisions can have the effect of redistributing funds to pupils who, from a local perspective, have lower levels of 'need' than similar pupils who receive no extra support.

The potentially distorting influence of certain parents and 'conditions'

Early in the development of the tribunal, concerns were expressed that articulate parents would dominate the system (Fish and Evans, 1995; Bibby and Lunt, 1996). The annual reports of SENDIST do not at present provide information on the social background of the parents who appealed, so one is unable to see whether appeals are associated with parents of one social background or another.

Analyses of tribunal cases in the first year showed that the majority of the appeals were for dyslexia. It appeared that LEAs were having to pay for expensive provision for a number of 'dyslexic' children, which distorted their spending on other areas of SEN provision (House of Commons, 1995). Subsequently, as the remit of autism was widened to comprise 'autistic spectrum disorder', there has been an increase in such cases referred to the tribunal.

It is not possible for the tribunal to relate in its annual report percentages concerning particular areas of SEN (e.g. specific learning difficulties, autism) with percentages of areas of SEN as they appear to exist nationally. National-level data are unavailable at present. However, when such data become available, if the tribunal were to employ them this would allow readers to see, for example, whether any areas of SEN appeared to be under or over-represented.

It is perhaps too optimistic to expect any parents to be very much concerned with other children when it comes to seeking extra money to support their own child. Theirs is not the responsibility to see that all children get a fair share of SEN and other funding: that is the duty of the LEA and others. So each parent may be expected to press for as much support and money as he or she can get. For each parent who successfully (from the parent's point of view) gains funding as a result of a tribunal decision, where this conflicts with any overall local system there are inevitably local implications. Such decisions may have an impact upon any local attempt at demonstrable, publicly agreed fairness in relation to locally agreed criteria and will distort parity with regard to local funding. It is in the light of such reservations that some involved in education continue to express the view that earlier concerns about parents and distortions of funding have been subsequently been substantiated (e.g. Evans and Gerber, 2000). If such influences are distorting in the sense that they reflect a disproportionate use of SENDIST, this is also likely to distort LEA attempts at parity in funding.

Thinking points

Practitioners may wish to consider:

- the advantages of initially focusing on the definitions of 'difficulty in learning' and 'disability' in the Education Act 1996;
- the benefits of developing and maintaining, within the legal framework, a clear, locally agreed definition of SEN shared by LEA officers, schools, parents and others;
- tensions between the SENDIST individualised approach and the broader LEA approaches to support and funding for pupils with SEN; and
- whether, in consultation with parents and others, anything further can be done locally to make funding broadly equitable (i.e. fair and transparent) while allowing flexibility to provide for the individual differences of pupils with SEN.

▌ Key texts

Department for Education and Skills (DfES) (2001a) *Special Educational Needs Code of Practice*. London: DfES.
  Especially useful for the legal definition of SEN taken from the Education Act 1996 and for the various sections mentioned in this chapter relating to forms of support and the graduated approach.
Farrell, M. (2001) *Standards and Special Educational Needs*. London: Continuum.
Especially Chapters 1, 2 and 3.
Special Educational Needs and Disability Tribunal (annually) *Annual Report*. London: SENDIST.

4

Political Judgements, Inclusion and the Future of Special Schools

Introduction

This chapter considers the issues and information that are important when forming political judgements about the future role of local special schools. The chapter first illustrates the contested nature of the concepts of social justice, equal opportunity and discrimination. It then considers that aspect of inclusion which regards education outside the mainstream as discriminatory and it looks at trends in the numbers of pupils educated in special schools. Issues are examined relating to making political judgements about the future of local special schools and their role. These include:

- the context of international reports on inclusion;
- the *Report of the Special Schools Working Group* (DfES, 2003);
- parental views; and
- the relative achievement of pupils in particular mainstream schools and special schools.

Social justice, equal opportunities and discrimination

It is necessary to set a context for a discussion on special schools and their role by looking at the concepts of equal opportunity and discrimination and how these relate to aspects of inclusion.

Social justice as 'fairness'

In his 'justice as fairness' theory, Rawls (1971) presents principles that, he argues, people would endorse if they were deprived of knowledge of their own social status and position. In a hypothetical situation in which someone is deprived of any knowledge about his or her own abilities, should that person be given a choice of whether to live in an egalitarian society or an inegalitarian one, he or she would be likely to choose to live in a egalitarian society. This is because the hope of being rich would be countered by the fear of being poor, which would persuade that person behind the veil of ignorance of his or her own abilities to choose a society that is 'fair'.

For Rawls, social inequality is justified only when it has the effect of benefiting the least advantaged by improving incentives and increasing the size of the social pot. People co-operating for mutual advantage are entitled to equal claims for the results of their co-operation. They should not be penalised because of factors over which they have no control, such as genetic inheritance (or race or gender). Redistribution is a 'just' procedure because it conforms to a widely held view of what is fair. Equality of opportunity may be similarly justified.

A 'rights' theory of social justice and equal opportunities

Nozick's (1974) 'rights' view of social justice and equality of opportunity follows from his essentially libertarian conception of the state. He seeks to demonstrate that an 'ultra-minimal' state (having a monopoly over the use of force in a territory) emerges from a system of 'private protection associations'. The ultra-minimal state is transformed into a 'minimal' state (which involves redistribution for the 'general provision' of protective services) (1974: 52). Nozick argues that the transitions leading from the state of nature to the ultra-minimal state to the minimal state are morally legitimate, and the minimal state itself is morally legitimate (ibid.: 53, 113–19). No state more powerful or more extensive than the minimal state is legitimate or justifiable. Therefore such developments as 'social justice/redistributive justice' and 'equality of opportunity' (which go further than the minimal state) are neither legitimate nor justifiable.

Nozick sets out an entitlement theory of justice, seeing justice not as about equality but about individual property rights. Someone justly acquiring a property is entitled to it. Someone acquiring property through 'just' transfer (from someone else who is legitimately entitled to it) is entitled to the property (ibid.: 150).

Among Nozick's criticisms of Rawls' position is that Rawls appears to believe that everyone has some entitlement to the totality of natural assets as a 'pool', with no one having differential claims. The distribution of natural abilities is seen as a collective asset. Nozick accepts that, in a free society, people's talents do benefit others and not just themselves. What he questions is the extracting of even more benefit to others, asking 'is it so implausible to claim that envy underlies this conception of justice . . . ?' (ibid.: 229).

Meritocracy, equality and discrimination

Cavanagh (2002) considers the issues of meritocracy, equality and discrimination in relation to the question of how jobs should be fairly allocated. However, to some degree, his arguments have relevance to the issue of equality of opportunity in relation to SEN. He believes that there are circumstances in which one can justify constraining what people do with their 'property'. For example, suppressing racial hatred might be a reason for restricting employers' hiring and firing choices.

For Cavanagh, the notion of equality of opportunity is caught between the idea of meritocracy (being more deserving) and the view that circumstances should be arranged so that every one has an equal chance of success (equal chances). But he suggests that, if natural ability forms part of what it means to be more deserving, the chances of success can never be equal. To reconcile this tension, a person's chance of succeeding has to concern a probability of succeeding based on ignorance of anyone's abilities. Equal chances cannot withstand information about ability, yet meritocracy requires this information.

Cavanagh discusses the kind of egalitarianism that starts from a belief in equality. One example of an attempt to find a common feature that justifies treating people equally concerns potential. The argument is that there is a gap between what one can achieve unaided when only provided with basic necessities (such as food and shelter) and what one can achieve given the best education and support. Because this gap in potential is universal (although the size of the gap varies), it may be taken as an aspect of humanity shared by every one and therefore a justification for treating people equally in the distribution of resources. Cavanagh's view is that such similarities are not sufficiently detached from differences (the fact that the gap is even bigger for some people than for others) to make a convincing case for preferring to emphasise the similarity rather than the difference (2002: 110). Therefore he rejects the notion of equality, arguing that it is not something that should be pursued either on its own or in combination with other values, such as meritocracy.

Discrimination, he suggests, is not best regarded as linked to equality of opportunity – that is, not treating people according to merit or unequally. It is better seen as treating people with undeserved contempt.

Equal opportunities in schools

It will be seen from the above that the notion of equality of opportunity is neither straightforward nor uncontested. The supposed relationship between equal opportunity and discrimination is also questioned.

In schools, the expression 'equal opportunities' may be used broadly in relation to groups identified according to SEN, race, gender, nationality, religion, social class, sexual orientation or some other characteristic. Equality of opportunity may be taken to mean various things, such as equality of access, equivalent experience, overcoming limitations or equality of outcome (Farrell, *et al.*, 1995). Efforts to provide equality of opportunity are reflected in such features as school aims and objectives; policies; staffing structures; curricular plans and organisation; pupil groupings; pupil records; and relationships within the school (Farrell, 1999).

In legal terms, the notion of 'discrimination' implies less favourable treatment based on a specified difference. For example, the Special Education Needs and Disability Rights in Education Act 2001 sets out what constitutes disability discrimination in education. Discrimination is taken to occur if a 'responsible body', such as a school, 'for a reason which relates to his disability' treats a disabled pupil 'less favourably than it treats or would treat others to whom that reason does not apply'. If the responsible body does treat a disabled pupil in such a way, it must show that the treatment is justified.

Trends in inclusion

That thread of inclusion which argues for a greater number of pupils to be educated in mainstream schools and consequently fewer pupils in non-mainstream settings such as special schools is sometimes presented as an example of equality of opportunity. Consequently, not providing for a child in a mainstream school is seen in terms of inequality, intolerance and discrimination.

The authors of the *Index for Inclusion* (published by the Centre for Studies in Inclusive Education) see in racism, sexism, classism, homophobia, bullying and disablism a common source of '*intolerance* to difference and the abuse of power both to create and perpetuate *inequalities*' (Booth *et al.*, 2000: 14, emphasis added). It follows from this view that making schools more inclusive may lead to staff challenging their own '*discriminatory* practices and attitudes'. The document views inclusion as a continuing process in which the school tries to respond to all pupils as individuals. Inclusion is seen as involving cultures, policies and practices in the school and its locality. Schools are required critically to examine what can be done 'to increase the learning and participation of the diversity of students within the school and its locality' (ibid.: 12).

One trend that runs counter to a broad conception of inclusion has been a growth in the exclusion of pupils from schools for disciplinary reasons. Also in conflict with inclusion are greater pressures from mainstream schools for statements of SEN (and the funding they entail) because of the perceived or real greater demands made by pupils with SEN. These trends have come to be regarded as schools' response to increasing pressure for accountability in their provision and learning outcomes (Norwich, 2000: 5).

Table 4.1 *Percentages of pupils with statements in special and mainstream schools in 1997 and 2002*

	Maintained special schools and PRUs	Mainstream schools	Independent schools
1997	40	57	3
2002	37	60	3

Source: DfES (2002c: 6).

On the other hand, a steady decline has been discerned in the proportions of pupils in special schools. This, it has been argued (ibid.), relates to expectations (backed up by legislation) to reinforce the responsibilities of mainstream schools for their provision for SEN though the *Special Educational Needs Code of Practice* (DfES, 2001a). However, this apparent steady decline in the proportion of pupils in special schools has to be interpreted with caution. A report published in 1999 indicated that, of the 242,300 pupils in England with statements of SEN, only 42% were in special schools, a proportion that had reduced over time. But this change in proportion appears to relate to an increase in the numbers of pupils with statements of SEN in mainstream schools. The numbers of pupils in special schools had in fact risen in the five years covered by the report, to a peak of 93,500 pupils (OfSTED, 1999(a)).

A more recent statistics bulletin indicates that similar care needs to be taken when considering percentages rather that the numbers of pupils in special schools. Table 4.1 indicates that the percentage of pupils with statements placed in special schools or pupil referral units fell between 1997 and 2002 from 40 to 37%. There was a corresponding increase in the percentage of pupils with statements educated in mainstream schools (DfES, 2002c: 6).

However, the *numbers* of pupils in special schools had not changed as much as these percentages might at first suggest. Table 4.2 shows the numbers of pupils in special schools and pupil referral units in 1997 and 2002.

Table 4.2 *Numbers of pupils in special schools and pupil referral units 1997 and 2002*

	Maintained special schools	Pupil referral units	Maintained special schools and PRUs
1997	92,561 (more on roll)	1,693 with statements	94,254
2002	90,288 (more on roll)	1,844 with statements	92,132

Source: DfES (2002c: 9, Table 1a).

These figures indicate a fall in pupil numbers in special schools of 2,273 in five years or, on average, 455 pupils per year. In addition to the pupils in maintained special schools there are 4,670 pupils in non-maintained special schools and a further 5,760 in independent special schools (DfES, 2003: 172). Also, these figures do not take account of the numbers of pupils that are being taught in predominantly separate units in mainstream schools.

Political judgements about the future role of local special schools

Political judgements

To understand the context of special educational provision, it has been suggested that one needs to recognise the interaction and balance of social forces. This places special education within a national political context where, to a considerable degree, legislation, funding and social policy influence what happens within local areas and within neighbourhood schools (Norwich, 2000: 6).

When LEA officers (in close consultation with schools, parents and others), consider the future of special schools in their area and their possible role, several issues might inform the debate. Among these are the following:

- International reports on inclusion.
- The implications of *The Report of the Special Schools Working Group* (DfES 2003).
- Parental views of local mainstream and special schools.
- The relative performance of local mainstream and special schools.

International reports on inclusion

If local considerations about the future and the role of special schools are to be informed by the context of international reports on inclusion, the important documents include the following:

- The UN *The Rights of the Child* (United Nations, 1993).
- The *Salamanca Statement* (ONESCO, 1994).
- The UNESCO *Survey on Special Needs Education Law* (1996).

Article 23 of the UN *The Rights of the Child* (United Nations, 1993) states that 'children should be helped to become as independent as possible and to be able to take a full and active part in everyday life.' Similarly, the *Salamanca Statement* called upon governments to adopt (as a matter of policy or law) the principles of inclusive education and to enroll children in ordinary schools 'unless there were compelling reasons for doing otherwise' (UNESCO, 1994: 44). This, of course, leaves individual governments to decide what those compelling reasons are. In England, they relate to parental preference, avoiding harming the education of other pupils and, for individual schoools (but not in the same way for LEAs), the efficient use of resources.

The UNESCO *Survey on Special Needs Education Law* (1996) recognises that the principle of school-based integration acknowledges that some children have such disabilities and/or learning difficulties that education in a special school is necessary. Most countries reviewed in the report express similar provisos to educate some children in special schools. For instance, in Spain education in a special school is only authorised if the pupil's needs are not met in a mainstream school. In New Brunswick, Canada, 'exceptional pupils' must be placed in the same classroom as 'non-exceptional' pupils so long as this is not detrimental to the needs of the child. Icelandic law states that disabled pupils should be educated with non-disabled peers whenever possible.

The implications of *The Report of the Special Schools Working Group*

A multidisciplinary working group was establish to looked at the future role of special schools (DfES, 2003). Considering that special schools have made progress in outreach activities and in supporting the government's inclusion agenda, the group provided advice on how best to develop and clarify further the role of all special schools. These included LEA-maintained, independent and non-maintained special schools. The group concentrated on practical mechanisms to help special schools to operate more effectively, considering what might be done to enhance the prestige of special schools and to celebrate their achievements.

The group made recommendations relating to leadership, teaching and learning, funding and structures, and support beyond the classroom. Among the recommendations on leadership was that the National College for School Leadership should consider how to raise standards for the National Qualification on Headship to make sure they reflect the new role of special and mainstream schools and the wider inclusion agenda. Teaching and learning recommendations included that the use of the P-scales should be promoted, particularly in mainstream schools (ibid.: 9).

Regarding funding and structures, the group proposed that the DfES should consult with SEN Regional Partnerships and carry out an audit of provision and services across regions to identify gaps in provision. In the light of the audit, the DfES should promote regional centres of expertise to extend and improve educational practice for children with SEN across a particular area. The DfES should promote collaborative working between special and mainstream schools through twinning arrangements, federations and clusters (ibid.: 10).

Turning to support beyond the classroom, among the recommendations is that the Disabled Children's External Working Group within the National Service Framework (NSF) should consider measures to link special schools to initiatives emerging from the NSF (ibid.: 11).

In general, the report envisages more headteachers and teachers choosing to join the special school sector because it is one 'with a secure and long term future' (ibid.: 12, para. 17).

Parental views of local mainstream and special schools

Tens of thousands of parents express a preference for a special school over a mainstream school, and for many reasons. Some consider mainstream schools to be unwelcoming (e.g. Audit Commission, 2002: 2, para. 4). Others expect their child to make better progress in the local special school.

Among the 3,000 parents who responded to the consultation on the SEN green paper (DfES, 1997a), for every one parent who favoured manstream school, twenty favoured special schools. In cannot be assumed that these parents were a cross-section of all parents, but the strength of commitment is evident. Some parents believed that their child would be bullied in mainstream, and this could be a reason for encouraging mainstream inclusion in an effort to tackle the root causes of any intollerance. Other reasons were that, even if mainstream schools offered more opportunities than special schools, the response should be not to transfer pupils to mainstream but to enhance special schools. There was also disaffection with the percieved levels of resourcing, staff training, awareness and understanding in mainstream schools. Special schools were seen as centres of shared knowledge and expertise in teaching pupils with severe and complex SEN (summary in Wearmouth, 2000: 22).

In a local context, where the views of parents are taken into account, parents may be informed by the relative performance of local mainstream and special schools in raising the achievement of pupils with SEN.

SEN pupils' achievement in mainstream and special schools

It has been claimed that young people with SEN experience a narrower curriculum, while other factors (such as teachers' lower expectations) often constrain pupils' performance (Barnes *et al.* 1999: 107). If there is any truth in this view, the existence of a National Curriculum is one way of judging whether any pupils are receiving inappropriately a narrower curriculum than others, and this is raised in Office for Standards in Education (OfSTED) reports, if appropriate, for schools to take action on. Teachers' expectations

Table 4.3 *Percentage of pupils obtaining one or more grades A–Gs GCSE examinations in (1995 and 1996)*

	Mainstream schools	Special schools
1995	91.25	15.32
1996	93.40	16.29

Source: Secondary School Performance Tables (DfEE, 1995, 1996).

are again a feature monitored by OfSTED inspectors and where in any school this is low (in relation to the prior achievement of the pupils) the school must take action to put it right.

The fact that special schools enter fewer than a third of their pupils for General Certificate of Secondary Education (GCSE) examinations has been described as the outcome of a 'systematic disabling process' and of a 'denial of examination opportunities'. This view, expressed by Thomas (1997), was derived from his consideration of the 1995–6 *Secondary School Performance Tables* (DfEE, 1995: 1996). These tables report examination results from 3,985 mainstream and 1,028 special schools. Table 4.3 indicates the much lower performance of pupils in special schools compared with that of pupils in mainstream schools in relation to achieving one or more grade A–Gs in GCSE examinations.

Similarly, the percentage of pupils in Year 11 obtaining five or more grade A–Gs in GCSEs in 1996 was 87% in mainstream schools and 4% in special schools. Thomas (1997) concludes from this that, given the diverse population in special schools, success in examinations would be 'expected to be higher'. He speculates that special schools may be unable to provide adequate curriculum support for the wide range of pupils they teach in Year 11.

However, such conclusions ignore a crucial factor in interpreting such figures – the prior achievement of the pupils. If special schools are educating pupils with lower levels of attainment when they entered the school, the achievements of these pupils could only legitimately be compared with that of pupils with similar levels of achievement on entering mainstream schools. The results each obtains in GCSEs could then be meaningfully compared. For reasons that are not apparent, this was not done; neither was the pupils' attainment considered in any other form of accreditation.

Fortunately, where local debate concerns the future role of special schools, a more rigorous assessment of their relative performance can be made. As approaches to the issue of relative performance develop (e.g. Farrell, 2001: 33–5), there is clearer evidence of the standards reached by mainstream and special schools with regard to pupils with SEN (see Case Study 4.1).

Target setting and benchmarking, supported by appropriate forms of assessment, are an important part of the process of monitoring and evaluating standards of pupil attainment and progress. The Qualification and Curriculum Authority (QCA) performance descriptors, or P-scales (e.g. DfEE, 2001e), are an example of a form of assessment suitable for pupils working below Level 1 of the National Curriculum. Since December 2001, all schools have to set measurable targets at Key Stages 2, 3 and 4 using the P-scales or other performance criteria. (The University of Durham is currently collecting national data on the P-scales to provide schools with data from larger cohorts than would otherwise be available.) Case Study 4.1 indicates how an LEA can provide information on the relative progress of pupils with SEN in mainstream and special schools.

Case Study 4.1 *Hampshire LEA's work on the P-scales*

Hampshire LEA operates a sophisticated system of data collection and mathematical modelling drawing on assessments of pupils using the P-scales and National Curriculum levels. Pupils with statements of SEN, who attend either special schools or special units/resources provision based in mainstream schools, are tested annually. Data are also collected for many pupils in mainstream primary schools using P-scales for those with statements of SEN, thus allowing comparisons to be made of progress in mainstream and special schools. The LEA then collates this information (and has done so since 2000) to produce mathematically modelled 'trendlines' for the county.

Additionally, the progress data are published (from 2003 in a standardised way), thus allowing a school to see how a specific pupil progressed in relation to an average child of the same age with the same SEN. The data also enable a school to see, for example, whether its Key Stage 1 pupils with SEN progressed more in, say, English than was typical across the county.

This information is available separately for pupils with severe learning difficulties and moderate learning difficulties. It has not proved viable to extend this approach as robustly to other aspects of SEN (e.g. autism, emotional and behavioural difficulties, speech and language difficulties) either because of wide discrepacies in performance level or because of the small number of pupils on which this analysis would be based. For each of these 'areas' of SEN, trends are indicated for subsections of the P-scales: PSHE – attention; independent organisational skills; interacting; mathematics – shape, space and measure; using and applying (mathematics); English – listening; speaking; writing; and reading.

For each area of SEN (e.g. severe learning difficulties) trendlines are produced for pupils scoring at a level at which:

- only the lowest 5% score;
- only the lowest 25% score;
- 50% of pupils score;
- only the highest 25% score; and
- only the highest 5% score.

These trendlines indicate the attainment of pupils from 4 to 18 years old.

One way of using the data is to identify an individual pupil's starting point in a particular year (e.g. P-scale level 2 in Year R) and to determine the trendline of best fit.

This can then be used as a basis for setting subsequent targets and for judging added value above the county trend. This can be done either for individual pupils or for groups of pupils in mainstream or special schools. The data can be analysed in various ways to explore the differential progress of groups (e.g. by gender or ethnicity).

Importantly, the information can be used to judge the relative progress of pupils in mainstream and special schools, thus allowing the LEA, schools and parents to make evidence-based judgements about the cost benefits of inclusion.

LEA issues for further development include moderating the judgements of teachers about P-levels. Exemplars have already been provided across the subjects for P-scales 1 to 8.

Source: Based on information kindly supplied by Hampshire LEA.

Case Study 4.2 shows how a special school can demonstrate the progress its pupils have made. The information provided in Case Studies 4.1 and 4.2 (should it be desired), could inform judgements about the respective roles of mainstream and special schools.

Case Study 4.2 *Riverside School's use of P-scales and National Curriculum assessments for school target setting*

Riverside School in Waterlooville, Hampshire (a special school for pupils with moderate learning difficulties), uses P-scales and National Curriculum (NC) test and task assessments for various purposes. The school tracks the performance of pupils over an extended period of several years in reading, writing, speaking, listening, number, using and applying mathematics, shape and space, interaction, independence and attention. Trendlines are used to indicate the predicted achievement of individual pupils. This is used to inform target setting for the pupil, and the subsequent performance of the pupil is compared with the target.

The school compares the performance of pupils from year to year both individually and as a year group and as a whole-school cohort. It sets targets for subsequent years based on the pupil's earlier progress. These are expressed in terms of the percentage of pupils to reach a specified level on the P-scales or on NC tests and tasks. Targets are set at three levels to focus on lower, middle and higher-attaining pupils. For example, in Year 6 in mathematics targets have been set relating to a percentage of pupils reaching level 2B of the NC, a larger percentage reaching level 1A of the NC and a still larger percentage reaching level P8. For other aspects of achievement, targets may be set exclusively in terms of P-scales.

The progress towards targets and their achievement is linked appropriately with the school improvement priorities which are in turn linked in a systematic and formal way to staff performance management. As part of the performance management process, the teacher identifies which of the school improvement priorities he or she will focus on. The teacher then quantifies the progress to be made for the class group and agrees which teaching strategies, approaches, etc., will be implemented in the classroom to help the teacher achieve the pupil targets. The target-setting framework involves long-term, medium-term and short-term planning and, at the short-term planning level, individual education plans (IEPs) reflect the broader year and whole-school target-setting process.

School improvement priorities in a sense work to raise standards of pupil achievement from another dirrection. They specify an area in which the school aims to improve, and this is related in turn to performance management, target setting and IEPs to help ensure that it is achieved.

Source: Based on information kindly supplied by Riverside School, Waterlooville.

Thinking point

Practitioners may wish to consider reviewing pragmatically the developing role of the special school as government intentions unfold.

Key text

Department for Education and Skills (DfES) (2003) *The Report of the Special Schools Working Group*. London: DfES.
This report is expected to inform government policy towards special schools.

5

Ethical Issues

Introduction

This chapter illustrates some of the moral issues in preventing and treating disabilities and learning difficulties. First, it considers ethical issues relating to genetic screening services and people with disabilities and learning difficulties. It describes the technologies of preimplantation genetic diagnosis (PGD) and prenatal testing, the service of genetic counselling and the legal position regarding PGD and abortion. The chapter examines arguments for and against genetic screening and considers whether such procedures imply a devaluing of the lives of existing disabled people. Finally, the chapter briefly considers ethical issues relating to controversial treatments for children with learning difficulties and disabilities.

Genetic technologies, genetic screening and disability

Among the most difficult current ethical issues are those relating to genetic technology and genetic testing in relation to disability and difficulties. Before considering these, however, it is necessary to set out the procedural and legal background. This section therefore outlines:

- preimplantation genetic diagnosis (PGD);
- prenatal testing;
- genetic counselling; and
- the law on PGD and abortion.

Preimplantation genetic diagnosis

Preimplantation genetic diagnosis (PGD) enables embryos to be selected or rejected according to whether a gene fault is evident before a pregnancy is established. The technique combines *in vitro* fertilisation (IVF) and genetic testing. IVF involves fertilising the woman's egg outside her body in a laboratory so that the egg develops into an embryo. Several embryos are created in this way and tested for genetic defect. The faulty ones are rejected and up to three embryos (without the genetic defect) can be implanted in the womb. (Before this, the woman is given hormone injections, which stimulate the ovaries so that several eggs mature, rather than the usual single egg, each of which can be artificially fertilised.)

Inherited disorders that have been the subject of testing include the following:

■ Cystic fibrosis, a disease in which there is a tendency to chronic lung infections and an inability to draw certain nutrients from food.
■ Sickle cell anaemia, a blood disease occurring mainly in black people in which abnormal red blood cells lead to a chronic, severe reduction in the capacity of the blood to carry oxygen.
■ Huntington's disease, a condition characterised by jerky, involuntary movements and progressive mental impairment.

PGD has been used with people with a family history of such disorders so they can avoid the birth of further children with the condition.

Some genetically linked diseases associated with a faulty X chromosome are amenable to testing where carried by females only. Females have two X chromosomes while males have one X and one Y chromosome. Consequently males will be affected by any faulty X chromosomes and will go on to develop any inherited disease.

A female may carry the disease yet be healthy herself because of the presence of two X chromosomes. However, females may carry the disease and also be affected (for example, in the case of fragile X syndrome, one third of female carriers show some intellectual impairment).

For X-linked disorders, laboratory embryos can be tested and female-only ones implanted in the womb to reduce or eliminate the possibility of the embryo being affected. Among the disorders for which tests are carried out are the following:

■ Fragile-X syndrome, a defect of the X chromosome mainly affecting males that causes intellectual impairment and, in males, a tendency to epilepsy.
■ Haemophilia, a bleeding disorder almost exclusively affecting males. It is caused by a deficiency in a blood protein (factor VIII).
■ Duchenne muscular dystrophy, a disorder, that exclusively affects males and in which there is a progressive degeneration of muscle fibres. The disease often leads to death in the teenage years owing to heart failure or chest infection.

Prenatal testing

There are other ways in which couples might choose to avoid having a child with an inherited disorder. Having considered the risks of conceiving a child with such a condition, they may choose to conceive and then determine as early as possible in the pregnancy whether or not the child does in fact have the disorder. They then have the choice of whether or not the woman has an abortion. Examples of prenatal tests are:

- an ultra sound scan;
- chorionic villus sampling;
- amniocentesis; and
- a transnuchal scan.

An ultrasound scan is used for routine purposes, including checking if the foetus is alive. However, an ultrasound scan performed for routine purposes at around 12 weeks' gestation can also detect very serious abnormalities and defects. At 18–20 weeks' gestation, it is used to check if the foetus has developmental problems, such as defects of the spinal cord or heart.

Chorionic villus sampling (CVS) involves analysing tissue samples obtained from the placenta (which contains foetal cells) via a tube passed through the cervix (the neck of the uterus) or via a hollow needle inserted into the wall of the abdomen.

In amniocentesis, fluid is drawn from the sac around the foetus by inserting a hollow needle through the wall of the abdomen. Foetal cells in the fluid are analysed to detect such conditions as the following:

- Down's syndrome, a chromosome abnormality typified by intellectual impairment and in which a quarter of children have a heart defect at birth and experience a higher-than-average incidence of congenital deafness and acute leukaemia.
- Tay–Sachs disease, a metabolic disorder characterised by such signs as blindness, dementia, seizures and paralysis and which often leads to death before a child reaches the age of 4 years.

A transnuchal or nuchal translucency scan is a high-resolution ultrasound scan used to detect so-called 'markers' that may indicate Down's syndrome. These include translucency caused by the thickening of a layer of fluid in the nuchal area (that is, the nape of the neck).

One of the commonest uses of prenatal testing is to detect Down's syndrome (Hadley, 1996). Screening tests in early pregnancy indicate the likelihood a foetus may have Down's syndrome. The mother is then offered chromosome analysis. Foetal cells are sampled through amniocentesis or

CVS. Should chromosome analysis confirm that the foetus has trisomy 21 (the indicator of Down's syndrome), the parents may consider terminating the pregnancy. The mother then has the choice of abortion, of which there were 347 relating to Down's syndrome in England and Wales in 2001 (Department of Health, 2002: 31, Table 23).

Genetic counselling

Genetic counselling is provided by a general practitioner, a paediatrician or a clinical geneticist to someone considering having a child but who is concerned about inherited diseases. Such people may have a blood relative with an inherited disorder (perhaps a previous child), or they may be at risk of bearing a child with an inherited disorder for some other reason.

Often, genetic counselling involves predicting the likelihood of a condition recurring that has already affected a family member. It may involve discussing the likely development of any affected child. It may also entail advising couples about contraception should they decide not to have children (or, if they already have children, should they decide not to have any more).

The law on PGD and abortion

PGD procedures fall under the remit of the Human Fertilisation and Embryology Act 1990, which regulates all activities related to human embryos outside the body. This includes the creation of human embryos and their storage, as well as their use in *in vitro* fertilisation or for research. Clinics offering *in vitro* fertilisation services (including PGD) are licensed and inspected by the Human Fertilisation and Embryology Authority (HFEA). The HFEA was set up under the Human Fertilisation and Embryology Act 1990. A licensing committee of the HFEA determines (on a case-by-case basis) the genetic disorders and conditions for which centres can screen.

The legal position on abortion includes the option for the abortion of a foetus that is disabled or has a 'serious handicap'. Mary Stopes International points out that among the reasons why women have abortions are 'having financial problems', 'not wanting children at all' and 'having a pregnancy that will result in a seriously handicapped baby' (Donellan, 2000: 1).

The (indirect) legislation relating to prenatal testing is the Abortion Act 1967 (as amended). Following the diagnosis of a genetic condition in the foetus, a woman can request an abortion. A legal abortion is one that takes place up to 24-weeks' gestation when two doctors agree that continuation of the pregnancy threatens the physical or mental health of the woman or that of her existing children. An abortion is also legal if the foetus is diagnosed as at substantial risk of serious abnormality, in which case the 24-week time limit does not apply. Professional bodies (such as the Royal College of Obstetricians and Gynaecologists) provide guidelines of good practice for prenatal screening and diagnosis.

Issues concerning genetic screening

It is self-evident that certain moral judgements are implicit in the procedures and laws relating to genetic screening and abortion. For example, the time limit on legal abortions of 24 weeks may be taken to suggest that the earlier an abortion takes place, the more morally acceptable it is. A point is reached where the viability of the foetus is such that it is less morally acceptable to have an abortion. The arbitrary cut-off point of 24 weeks could be claimed to be a manifestation of this moral position.

Perhaps more pertinent to the theme of this chapter is that a moral judgement concerning 'serious abnormality' is implied by the fact that the 24-week time limit does not apply to the abortions when the foetus is diagnosed as at substantial risk of such serious abnormality. Further ethical judgements are involved in the decisions of the licensing committee of the HFEA.

Some of the arguments against genetic screening are listed below. Genetic screening is immoral because it:

- promotes an irresponsible attitude towards reproductive behaviour;
- promotes negative views of existing disabled people;
- diverts resources away from removing disabling 'barriers' in society; and
- ignores the innate value and complexity of human life.

To take these arguments in turn, it has been argued that genetic testing locates the birth of disabled children within the remit of reproductive choice, thus making it possible to accuse parents of having an irresponsible attitude towards reproductive behaviour (Reinders, 2000: x). To counter this argument, it could be claimed that social welfare should be a safety net that is more cost effective than a more comprehensive welfare state, and that such a minimalist safety net should encourage people to accept responsibility for their own actions. If so, it follows that people should take responsibility for reducing social costs (including in the area of reproductive choice) by avoiding the birth of children with disabilities.

It is also claimed that the abortion of foetuses that have a particular disability may promote negative attitudes towards people who are already alive and who have the same disability. For example, the termination of a pregnancy because the foetus is likely to be 'deaf' or, in PGD diagnosis, rejecting 'deaf' embryos can be seen as part of a more general negative attitude towards deaf people (Fletcher, 2002: 23). Similarly, if someone wishes to prevent bringing into the world a child with a genetic condition, a contributing factor might be his or her negative image of existing people with such a conditions. Preventative strategies imply, at least indirectly, a negative view of the lives of existing people with disabilities 'because without such evaluations these strategies could not make sense' (Reinders, 2000: 9).

If the medical model of disability prevails, this could reduce the importance of social understandings of disabilities and learning difficulties. It has therefore been suggested that, if less attention is given to social understandings of disability, fewer resources will be devoted to 'non-genetic methods' of improving the quality of children's health (English and Sommerville, 2002: 10). Similarly, the International League of Societies for Persons with Mental Handicap (1994: 11) has expressed concern that efforts and resources they believe would be better spent on removing disabling barriers in society (such as difficulty of physical access and negative attitudes) could be diverted to genetic research.

It may be argued that every life is of value and that the diversity of humans as a species has some kind of innate value. Some take the view, therefore, that, for most people affected by impairments, it is the attitudes of others or barriers to participation in society that are the determining factors affecting their quality of life. Every effort, therefore, should be put into changing society so that it embraces human differences. The International League of Societies for Persons with Mental Handicaps (ibid.: 7) cite certain commonly held assumptions they consider put people with disabilities at risk with regard to genetic and reproductive technology. These include:

■ people with disabilities suffer because of their disability;
■ human value is judged in terms of a particular person's intellectual or physical qualities;
■ the human race can and should be improved; and
■ genetic factors are the main or sole consideration when understanding differences between people.

Some of the arguments in favour of genetic screening are listed below. Genetic screening is acceptable because it:

■ can improve the life chances of existing people with disabilities;
■ is better that children are born healthy rather than sick or disabled;
■ involves a personal not a social choice (the treatment of disease is a separate issue from the good of society);
■ is selection not *against* disability but *for* the advantages of a normal life.

The first-ever use of PGD, indicates its potential to improve the life chances of other disabled people. An embryo that became Adam Nash was genetically selected by PGD to ensure that it did not have the gene fault for Fanconi's anaemia (a serious, sometimes fatal condition) Adam's sister suffered from. After Adam was born (without the condition), he became his sister's blood donor, thus doubling her chances of survival (Lee, 2002: xi).

Genetic screening, it may also be claimed, does not imply that people with a genetic disease should never be born but that, all other things being equal, it is preferable that a child is born healthy rather than sick or disabled. For example, in Sardinia, the blood disorder thalassaemia (a wasting disease usually leading to heart failure) was once prevalent. Each year about 100 babies were born with the condition. However, in 1974, a screening programme was launched that offered abortions to women with affected pregnancies. Now only four or five babies with thalassaemia are born each year, thus preventing the birth of many babies who would have suffered a diseased life and an early death (Konner, 1993). Genetic screening, therefore, gives people who are aware they carry a genetic disease a chance to give birth to healthy children. Many might otherwise never risk pregnancy or would immediately choose to have an abortion if they accidentally became pregnant (Hadley, 1996: 121).

It has been argued that parents who already have a disabled child and who decide to terminate an affected foetus can continue to love the existing child while not wanting their next child to have the same condition. Also, such parents may consider they are making a personal choice and that their decision is not necessarily one they would wish to generalise to the rest of society (Tizzard, 2002: 39). Similarly, it may be claimed that, with regard to the life of an individual, it would be better not to suffer from a disease and that this would also be better in the long term for society as a whole. The question this raises is whether society should give precedence to alleviating individual suffering over such potential repercussions as devaluing the lives of existing people who have disabilities and learning difficulties.

While selecting genetically against disabilities may be seen as unfair discrimination against existing disabled people, such choices may also be presented as being not *against* disability but *for* advantages. Harris (2002) evokes a scenario in which some embryos have a genetic condition that gives them complete immunity to many major diseases, along with increased longevity. Given the choice, there would be moral reasons to prefer implanting such embryos. However, such a decision does not imply that the lives of people who are 'normal' at the time such immune genes are chosen are not worth living or that their quality of life is poor or problematic (ibid.: 57–8).

Does genetic screening devalue the lives of existing disabled people?

Some of the arguments against genetic screening relate more directly to the notion of devaluing the lives of existing disabled people. For example, the view that genetic screening encourages irresponsible reproductive behaviour suggests negative views of the parents of existing people who have disabilities and learning difficulties. However, such negative views of these parents is, it could be argued, at one remove from the negative view of the person their child is expected to become. However, screening can be seen as a form of discrimination against the embryo, as well as a form of discrimination against those who have the condition for which the embryo is rejected. In this way, some of the arguments against genetic screening are more directly relevant to the view that genetic screening implies a negative evaluation of the lives of existing people with disabilities and learning difficulties.

Among views supporting genetic screening, the point that it can improve the life chances of those with disabilities seems to argue against the devaluing of disabled lives. In the example of Adam Nash discussed earlier, it could be said this case devalued disabled lives because disabled embryos were rejected before the embryo that became Adam was implanted. However, the benefit to Adam's sister was an improvement in the quality of her life and a reduction in the impact of her condition. Unless one takes the view that even this devalues disabled lives because Adam's sister was not accepted as she is, it could be taken as an indirect example of improving, not devaluing, an existing person's life.

Controversial treatments

Among other ethical issues in special education are those relating to treatments considered to be controversial. An example is the use of drugs to treat various conditions. While it is rare to administer drugs to children in the UK who do not have physical illnesses or major psychiatric illnesses such as schizophrenia, in the USA this appears to be less so (Campbell and Cueva, 1995).

In the UK, efforts to treat emotional and behavioural difficulties arising in childhood have been constrained because of a concern about the long-term effects of drug treatments on a child. There is also an 'ethical dilemma' that, because childhood problems can be influenced by many factors, it is difficult to justify using drugs that suppress a symptom without identifying the cause of the problem (Elliot and Place, 1998: 26). For example, is it legitimate to ask whether it is morally right to treat a child's violent behaviour by drug treatment if that child's behaviour is a normal reaction to a family life that is itself violent and fractured? For such reasons it is unusual in the UK for drugs to be considered as the first line of treatment for emotional and behavioural difficulties.

There has, however, been continuing debate about the use of such medication as the stimulant Ritalin for children diagnosed as having attention deficit hyperactivity disorder (ADHD). It has been suggested that as many as 80% of children with ADHD respond favourably to medication (Lyon, 1994). However, it seems widely accepted that a thorough assessment is necessary before medication is used and that, when it is used, its effects should be carefully and continuously monitored (Wodrich, 1994). A further concern is that medication alone is not considered to lead to an improvement in a child's long-term academic performance, social behaviour and emotional development (Cooper and Ideus, 1995) (see Case Study 5.1).

Case study 5.1 *Using medication for attention deficit hyperactivity disorder*

James is 10 years old. His teachers have always described him as easily distracted. He has difficulty concentrating, is restless and lately his behaviour has seriously deteriorated. He was always thought of as a 'bright' child but the distractibility and restlessness have apparently interfered with his ability to learn the required academic, social and behavioural skills. He seems to get frustrated easily and his low self-esteem is often reflected in anger.

After a comprehensive evaluation ruled out other possible causes, he was eventually diagnosed as having attention deficit hyperactivity disorder. Stimulant medication was recommended. The clinician provided James's parents with information about ADHD and explained why James was having difficulty. He carefully explained why medication would be useful and that the benefits heavily outweigh any possible side-effects. He discussed the fact that the medication would only make James more available for learning and that he would still need support to help him with the skills he had not learnt.

James's parents were concerned that he needed medication to help him do what other children do easily. However, after considerable soul searching, they decided to put their personal concerns and fears aside and to look at what would be in the best interests of James. After an initial trial of medication, they observed a remarkable improvement in James's self-esteem. They realised the medication did not change James but that with appropriate support, he would have a better chance of achieving his potential.

Source: From information kindly provided by Dr Ronald Weinstein, Executive Director, Young Options Institute.

Difficulties in assessing treatments that are unproven present another ethical dilemma. Many treatments now considered as standard were once controversial but gradually became accepted as their efficacy was demonstrated in different circumstances and over a long period of time. On the other hand, the too-ready acceptance of unproven approaches (for example, on the part of parents of children with SEN) can lead to false hopes of a cure and a delay in following standard approaches that may be more beneficial for the child.

Hornby *et al.* (1997) review several controversial treatments, including conductive education, the use of Irlen lenses and the provision of facilitated communication. Conductive education is a system of education for children (and adults) with motor disorders (such as cerebral palsy) that was developed by Andras Peto at the Peto Institute in Hungary. Hornby *et al.*, however, conclude that conductive education has been shown to be less effective than existing treatments. Irlen lenses are a remedial technique involving coloured lenses for children with dyslexia. These lenses are considered to make reading easier by counteracting the light-sensitive conditions thought to effect some children. Little or no evidence has been found in favour of their effectiveness. Facilitated communication is a means of assisting non-verbal children to communicate using a keyboard or by pointing to a board containing an alphabet. While this technique has been used with children with autism, there has been little evidence of its effectiveness.

The implication is that professionals should communicate such findings to colleagues, educational administrators, policy-makers and parents of children with disabilities. This would help them to make suitable decisions about the education of children with SEN (ibid.: 183–4).

Thinking points

Practitioners may wish to consider further the basis of moral judgements relating to children with disabilities and difficulties regarding:

■ prevention;
■ diagnosis/identification; and
■ provision.

Key texts

Hornby, G., Atkinson, M. and Howard, J. (1997) *Controversial Issues in Special Education*. London: David Fulton.
This book considers controversial diagnoses (including autism), system-wide interventions (such as inclusion), group interventions (such as conductive education) and individual interventions (including facilitated communication).
Reinders, H.S. (2000) *The Future of the Disabled in Liberal Society: An Ethical Analysis*. Notre Dame, IN: University of Notre Dame Press.
A closely argued if, in parts, controversial analysis.

6

SEN Funding in a Redistributive Society

Introduction

This chapter explains the broad financial policies of Best Value in schools and of fair funding. It then turns to special education funding, focusing on the destination of the funding, forms of funding and the criteria for effective funding models. The chapter describes the elements of a recommended approach to special education financing, considering basic funding for all pupils, the additional educational needs element, school clusters, support services for pupils with complex needs and special schools. The question of evaluating provision and the continuing development of the National Performance Framework for SEN is touched on. Finally, the chapter looks critically at the identification of dyslexia and autistic spectrum disorder as being susceptible to economic pressures for more funding in a redistributive society as these disorders are not easy to define. It therefore emphasises the importance of local agreements concerning how such conditions are to be identified, assessed and provided for.

General funding issues

Best Value in schools

The government's Best Value policy (DfES, 2002a) is intended to encourage a continuous improvement in locally provided services. In schools it applies to raising the standards of pupils' attainment through, for example, better leadership. Best Value extends the value-for-money principles of economy, effectiveness and efficiency. It assumes that a partnership with those who are served by the school and the effective use of resources lead both to raising educational standards and to continuous improvement.

The principles of Best Value are to challenge, compare, consult and compete (ibid.: 3). These 'four Cs' are used either separately or in combination with each other. Challenge involves asking critically why, how and by whom an activity is carried out. The second principle refers to the school comparing its performance against that of other schools or comparing different parts of the same school. Consulting applies to involving pupils, parents and others. Competing is seen as a way of securing efficient and effective resources.

The Local Government Act 1999 introduced the policy of Best Value to help secure better value for money from local government services. Best Value is a statutory requirement for local authorities, who are expected to carry out regular reviews of their services using the four Cs to inform their judgements. It is not, however, a stautory requirement for schools, but governing bodies are required to set targets to raise standards and are expected to provide good-quality schooling and to spend public money wisely (ibid.: 4). The requirements for Best Value intermesh with those for fair funding, discussed below.

Fair funding

The School Standards and Framework Act 1998 made changes to the way schools are funded, delegating to schools a larger proportion of funds to spend than previously (DfEE, 1998c). As part of 'fair funding' (DfES, 2002b), schools are expected to follow the principles of Best Value when making decisions about major activities. LEA 'schemes for financing schools' (made under s. 48 of the School Standards and Framework Act 1998) require governing bodies, when they submit their annual budget plans to the LEA, to include what has come to be known as a 'Best Value statement'.

Fair funding is used by LEAs to calculate the budgets of the schools they maintain. It provides the framework for the financial relationship operating between schools and LEAs. Fair funding built on the earlier system of local management of schools (LMS), which related to formula funding and the delegation of financial responsibility to schools. Formula funding is intended to lead to the equitable allocation of resources between schools based on objectively measured needs. Consequently, within each LEA, schools with the same characteristics and the same number of pupils should be allocated the same level of resources under the LEA's formula. Delegation refers to the proportion of the LEA's total expenditure on schools which is allocated to the schools themselves in budget shares through the LEA's formula (rather than retained centrally by the LEA). An example of increased delegation is the provision for mainstream school pupils with statements of SEN. Previously, this provision was usually funded centrally by the LEA but, more recently, the relevant funding is being increasingly transferred to schools' delegated budgets.

Under the School Standards and Framework Act 1998, a new framework was established of community, voluntary and foundation schools. Fair funding was meant to complement the new schools framework by establishing a single system of funding which allows schools further to develop their capacity for self-government by increased delegation of responsibility through funding (DfES, 2002b: 2).

In 2003–4, the government planned to change LEA and school funding so that 'education standards spending assessments' would now deal separately with the spending needs of schools and those of the LEAs themselves. The school funding system was brought into line with the new LEA funding system by replacing the local schools budget (the starting point for fair funding) with separate school and LEA budgets that correspond to two spending needs assessments (ibid.: 5). This change was implemented.

Special education funding: budgets, funding and funding models

A study by the European Agency for Development in Special Needs Education (involving countries in the EU, Iceland and Norway) considered the financing of special education (Meijer, 1999). Among important factors with regard to budget allocation, the study focused on the following:

- The destination of the budget.
- Forms of funding.
- Criteria for effective funding models.

The *destination of budgets* refers to the agency that initially receives the budget and from which it may be reallocated for example, the pupil (parents), the school and school clusters/local resource centre.

Forms of funding were considered according to input, throughput and output. Input funding is part of the formula funding of schools. For example, the SEN element of a mainstream school budget may be calculated according to proxy indicators, such as eligibility for free school meals or end-of-key-stage attainment data. Special schools are often funded according to the number of places available. Throughput funding (such as service-level agreements), relates to developing or maintaining a service up to a certain specified level and performing certain activities or functions. Input and throughput funding often inter-relate (Fletcher-Campbell, 2002). For example, funds acquired by input funding may pay for agreed levels of service. Output funding involves schools or services acquiring funding for effectiveness once a task or activity is completed. This involves an analysis of the value added for pupils with SEN, highlighting factors that led to the successful output (for example, raising attainment in academic and social assessments as measured by performance descriptors). Up to specified levels, the factors that lead to successful outputs can be maintained by 'throughput funding'.

Criteria for effective funding models were one aspect of a project established by the DfES in September 2000 which concerned the distribution and delegation of resources to schools for SEN provision (Beek, 2002). These criteria included resource distribution for additional educational needs (AEN). Pupils with SEN were regarded as a group within a wider population of pupils who had AEN. The criteria set for evaluating the distribution of resources included models that should:

- support the inclusion of children with AEN in mainstream schools where possible;
- allow schools to manage the use and distribution of resources to aid efficiency;
- support early identification and intervention strategies;
- allow flexibility to meet the needs of children with particular, complex disabilities;
- be developed in partnership with schools and others; and
- involve accountability, including monitoring how resources are used and the outcomes for children.

A recommended approach

General comments

Drawing on developments such as those mentioned above, the DfES (2001c) provided guidance in the form of *The Distribution of Resources to Support Inclusion*. The approach recommended in the guidance considered, among other things:

- basic funding for all pupils;
- additional educational needs factors;
- cluster funding;
- support services;
- special school funding; and
- accountability.

Case Study 6.1 illustrates one approach to SEN funding for mainstream schools. The remainder of this section goes on to consider the listed elements of the DfES recommended approach.

Case Study 6.1 *Norfolk LEA funding for SEN in mainstream schools*

In Norfolk, the LEA has a single system of formula funding for SEN, for both non-statutory SEN and for pupils with statements of SEN. For pupils *with* statements, pupils assessed as having very high levels of SEN may be placed in 'band E'. Funds for these pupils are allocated according to the actual level of provision required. The assessment includes curriculum, behaviour and physical and medical care needs. Curriculum needs are assessed using standardised tests of reading and mathematics, except for children in the Reception year, who are assessed on the results of the Bury Infant Check. Statutory-aged pupils scoring below a certain level on the standardised tests, or who have been professionally diagnosed as having SEN, are further assessed using a curriculum checklist for primary pupils and a diagnostic curriculum test for secondary pupils.

Pupils *without* statements are assessed on the same basis as pupils with statements. Bandings are attributed on the basis of the actual scores in each of the assessed areas. The scores are calibrated each year to ensure that the distribution of funds equals the resources available. The assessment of curriculum, behaviour and physical and medical care needs is used to place pupils in one of the bands A–D. Each band carries a fixed level of funding which is given to the school to provide 'whole school' funding. The funding is not pupil specific.

Through a system of 'block allocation', a percentage of the SEN funding is distributed to all schools based on a three-year average of the number of pupils tested who score just below the requirement for band A (the lowest-funded band). For each child falling into this category, the school receives a fixed sum. This is also given to the school to provide 'whole school' funding.

Some schools have specific units for pupils with SEN. These units are funded on the basis of the numbers of pupils in them at a particular time. In addition to place-led funding, these units also receive fixed sums and may receive funding for notional pupils, depending on the numbers on roll. As the pupils are on the roll of the mainstream school in which the unit is based, they attract the appropriate age-weighted pupil allowance.

Schools with high levels of social deprivation receive additional funds according to three-year average levels of entitlement to free school meals at each particular school.

Source: From information kindly provided by Norfolk LEA.

Basic funding for all pupils

Basic funding for all pupils is allocated through age-weighted pupil units and other factors that are applied to all schools. Other funds and grants may add to the school's income. For example, under the Standards Fund, resources can be allocated under the heading 'inclusion' to:

- support the SEN training and professional development of teachers and other staff;
- support the introduction of parent partnership and conciliation services for parents of children with SEN;

- develop and support inclusive education systems by enabling more placements of pupils with SEN in mainstream settings and supporting special school outreach work; and
- improve speech and language therapy provision for children with communication difficulties.

Basic funding should support the costs of all the normal teaching and learning arrangements within a school, including SENCO time. Also, the curriculum should be differentiated to provide suitable learning opportunities for most pupils. It is expected that basic funding resources should support many pupils at School Action level (DfES, 2001c: para. 8.2.2).

The additional educational needs element

Another element of school funding (which complements basic funding) that is allocated according to local formulae is the additional educational needs (AEN) element. This may involve the use of proxy or direct indicators. Proxy indicators are used by LEAs to allocate resources for the social needs of pupils with AEN (but without statements of SEN). These indicators include:

- the number of pupils on the school roll;
- eligibility for free school meals;
- key stage attainment data (perhaps based on average results over several years);
- some form of 'baseline' assessment;
- reading test scores; and
- mobility and turbulence factors.

Direct indicators may involve a pupil audit. Resources are distributed according to the assessed needs of individual pupils, often using locally agreed criteria to determine a resource band for each eligible pupil. Each band is associated with an amount of money that is delegated to schools. A moderating system may be used, involving headteachers or SENCOs.

There may be a formula that allocates funds according to both proxy indicators and direct pupil audit and, perhaps, other factors. There should also have been consultation between LEAs and schools to establish a system all consider fair. The purpose of allocating funds through such direct and proxy indicators is to ensure that schools which have relatively more pupils from disadvantaged backgrounds receive more funding.

The AEN element is not solely for pupils with SEN but for others, including travellers and pupils in public care. AEN resources should:

- allow greater differentiation of the curriculum;
- contribute towards the cost of additional teaching equipment and materials;

- support teaching and learning in smaller classes or in groups; and
- provide occasionally for some individual teaching or support (DfES, 2001c: para. 8.3.1).

Pupils with 'moderate learning, behavioural or health-related needs' should be fully supported by basic budget and AEN funding. It should be possible to meet the needs of most pupils at School Action and School Action Plus levels from the same resources but supplemented by other specific funding, such as Standards Fund social inclusion grants and ethnic minority and traveller achievement grants. (ibid.: para. 8.3.2).

School clusters

A funding approach that uses a school cluster model concerns pupils who will have complex learning and behaviour difficulties. The model involves the LEA allocating resources for those pupils to a group of schools and LEA officers. This group then distributes additional resources (according to agreed criteria) to supplement the resources already made available.

A moderation system is employed in this approach, perhaps involving SENCOS. Proxy indicators are sometimes used to allocate funds for pupils with SEN whose needs are not complex. The model does not require pupils to have statements of SEN in order to be able to attract resources.

Support services for pupils with complex needs

Funding held centrally by the LEA may be used to pay for support staff, such as advisory support teachers. Special schools may operate an outreach service that fulfils a similar role.

Special schools

Special schools are funded according to a combination of factors, such as the number of planned places; the complexity of pupils' needs; curriculum factors; and the services (such as outreach) the schools provide to others (see Case Study 6.2).

Case Study 6.2 *Norfolk LEA funding for SEN in special schools*

In Norfolk special schools, pupil places are allocated in five levels, according to the profile of the school identified in the annual pupil audit. The audit considers curriculum, care and behaviour needs.

Each pupil also attracts an allocation independent of need level. Special schools with high levels of deprivation receive additional funds. Also, to ensure the protection of the curriculum in special schools, each is allocated a fixed sum.

Source: From information kindly supplied by Norfolk LEA.

Evaluating provision and the National Performance Framework for SEN

The LEA should retain funds in order that it can support a system that reviews provision for pupils with SEN (or additional educational needs). In evaluating provision, the LEA and others take into account learning outcomes, the organisation of support and specialist teaching arrangements. There must be arrangements to make sure that the provision specified in pupils' statements is in place.

Against this background, the Special Educational Needs Division of the DfES is continuing to develop the National Performance Framework for SEN. It is intended that this framework will help LEAs to stop asking for data from schools that are already available elsewhere. The framework brings together key performance indicators to help LEAs with the process of self-review. It enables LEAs to use benchmarking data to set (and monitor) local targets to improve their performance in meeting the needs of pupils with SEN. The data include the following:

■ Social disadvantage indicators (an index of multiple deprivation and free school meals eligibility).
■ School and pupil population indicators (e.g. the number of pupils attending mainstream schools, special schools and pupil referral units).
■ SEN and early years indicators (such as the number of children under 5 years old with statements held by each LEA).
■ Inclusion indicators (such as the percentage of pupils in special and mainstream schools).
■ SEN population indicators (such as the number of pupils with SEN with and without statements in mainstream schools).

It is not clear whether the database will in the future include what is perhaps the most important information of all – that relating to the attainment of pupils with SEN.

Economic pressures for funding and the importance of locally agreed definitions

Throughout this chapter mention has been made of approaches that help to ensure fair and equitable local funding for schools. One factor that might work against this is the lack of clarity in identifying learning difficulties and disability, particularly in the case of so-called 'non-normative' SEN, such as dyslexia, emotional and behavioural difficulties and autistic spectrum disorder. This section therefore considers two examples of such non-normative SEN: dyslexia and autistic spectrum disorder.

Dyslexia

The *Special Educational Needs Code of Practice* (DFES, 2001a) does not offer a definition of dyslexia that would aid agreement about its identification. In considering the statutory assessment of SEN, the code refers to evidence of attainment and progress, stating that:

> An individual child's *attainment* must always be understood in the context of the *attainments* of the child's peers, the child's rate of *progress* over time and, where appropriate, expectations of the child's performance. A child's apparently weak performance may, on examination of the evidence, be attributable to wider factors associated with the school's organisation (ibid.: 7.39, emphasis added).

The phrase 'expectations of the child's performance' is problematic. It would seem to leave open the door for an unfair statutory assessment of a child as having SEN who reads at national age average level but was judged to be behind because of his or her very high performance in other areas of the curriculum. This would not, presumably, occur for a child who was average in all curriculum areas because his or her average reading would not be 'behind' other areas. It is therefore possible that a child who is only average in all curriculum subjects does not receive (rightly) a statutory assessment while a child who is attaining at the same level in reading and who is above average in many areas of the curriculum may receive a statutory assessment. And statutory assessment may, of course, lead to a funded statement of SEN.

A report by OfSTED (1999b) that involved a small-scale survey undertaken in 1997 and 1998 evaluated provision for pupils who were the subject of a statement of SEN in respect of specific learning difficulties (which the report, incorrectly, equates with dyslexia). Primary and secondary mainstream schools were visited. Most pupils attended specialist provision in units, classes, departments or resource bases attached to mainstream schools which provided mainly or wholly for pupils with specific learning difficulties. The focus was on the progress pupils made in learning to read, write and spell – these being the major weaknesses experienced by pupils with specific learning difficulties. The report states that these weakness, 'were evaluated in the overall context of pupils' performance in subjects across the curriculum' (ibid.: 5, para. 5).

The report notes that 'despite good teaching, the general attainment of the pupils was lower than expected for their chronological ages for two thirds of pupils in the final year of primary school and approximately half of the pupils in their final year of secondary school' (ibid.: main findings, para. 17).

This means that a third of the pupils in primary school and half of pupils in secondary school in the survey were achieving at a level in line with or better than their chronological age. However, it is not clear to what extent the achievement is dependent on support.

Referring to pupils at the end of the primary school phase, the report notes that, '[Even though] they were often reading at a level appropriate to their actual age by the time they transferred to secondary school, they still required help in developing higher-order reading, spelling and writing skills' (ibid.: 7, para. 34). In most cases, the pupils with specific learning difficulties were 'of average or below average ability, as measured by psychometric tests' (ibid.: 8, para. 40). In lessons, a third of primary-aged pupils and a half of secondary-aged pupils were performing at expected levels for the pupils' ages. In considering the progress of pupils, the report noted that 'progress in reading was such that their reading ages were approaching or even exceeding their chronological age' (ibid. p.9 para. 44). Yet no question was raised in the report about whether such children require a statement of SEN at all. Some LEAs had developed local criteria for determining whether a statement in respect of specific learning difficulties should be used. In most cases this was based on a disparity between the pupils' chronological age and their reading age, usually of two years or more (ibid.: 7 para. 35).

A report by the British Psychological Society (1999) also seems to take a view of dyslexia that would allow dyslexia to be defined in terms of a discrepancy in attainment, including a disceprepancy in average attainment in literacy with higher attainment in other areas. The report provides a working definition of dyslexia as evident when 'accurate and fluent word reading and/or spelling develops very incompletely or with great difficulty' (ibid.: summary, para. 2).

This working definition requires that three aspects are evaluated through assessment. First, assessment considers whether the pupil is learning or has learnt accurate and fluent word reading and/or spelling very incompletely. Secondly, there is an evaluation of whether appropriate learning opportunities have been provided. Finally, one assesses whether progress has been made only as a result of much additional effort and instruction and that the difficulties still persist (ibid.: summary, para. 7).

The report seeks to separate the identification of dyslexia from the assessment of SEN. While the identification of dyslexia draws on cognitive research and theory, SEN is seen as defined in relation to special educational provision. This allows for variation in SEN because provision that is considered to be special may vary between LEAs, schools and teachers. The report concludes that local policies largely determine cut-off points for the provision of special education within a continuum of what are considered mild, moderate or severe levels of dyslexia. The report considers that the working definition of dyslexia it adopts could be a starting point for social policy decisions. Features of the working definition (in particular, severity and persistence), taken together with other indicators, might inform an LEA's judgements about severe and long-term SEN (ibid.: summary, para. 10).

A potential difficulty with the BPS definition is the use of the expression, 'with great difficulty'. This could be taken to imply that a child may be considered to have dyslexia if he or she can read at the same level as other children of the same age but that 'it had been difficult'. It would surely be odd to consider a child as having, for example, severe learning difficulties and then say that the evidence for this is that the child works at the same level as other children of the same age. Evidence of severe learning difficulty is slow progress and lower attainment than other children.

Where there is variation in what constitutes dyslexia and at what level of significance reading, writing and spelling difficulties constitute a SEN, some parents may seek to argue for support and funding for their own child, with no reference to fairness to others. Indeed, it has been observed that it is 'an unhappy situation which allows the more vocal parents to achieve resources which may be equally needed by other pupils' (Hornby *et al.*, 1997: 48).

Autistic spectrum disorder

There has been an apparent increase in the prevalence of autistic spectrum disorders (ASD). Autism was originally considered to effect 0.025% of children (Humphries and Ramm, 1987). If the classic Kanner's syndrome and those with autistic features were included, the percentage was 0.045% (Lotter, 1966). An even broader definition of autism (which included those with social impairments characteristic of autism) produced a prevalence of 0.21% (Wing and Gould, 1979).

By 1992, the rate had increased to 0.23% when children with Asperger's syndrome are included (Aarons and Gittens, 1992). In December 2001, a report appropriately called *The Rising Challenge* (All Party Parliamentary Group on Autism, 2001) stated that 87% of LEAs perceived an increase in the number of children diagnosed with ASD over the previous five years. A likely reason was considered to be improvements in diagnosis and awareness. But 20% of LEAs thought there might be a 'real' increase in the condition. Also in December 2001, a Medical Research Council report found that, in every 10,000 children under the age of 8 years, 60 had autism. This is 0.6%. However, the report did recognise that factors that may give rise to an increase in prevalence over time include 'changing diagnostic thresholds'.

In 2002, the Autism Working Group produced good-practice guidance relating to autistic spectrum disorders (DfES/DH, 2002a; 2002b). In the guidance, ASD was taken to include individuals with a diagnosis of autism, autistic disorder, Kanner's or classical autism, childhood disintegrative disorder, Asperger's syndrome, pervasive developmental disorder, pervasive developmental disorder not otherwise specified, and semantic pragmatic disorder (DfES/DH, 2002a: 1.8). There is 'debate' concerning whether children with semantic pragmatic disorder and children with Asperger's syndrome are the same or different subgroups within the autistic spectrum (ibid: glossary p. 20).

The report refers to the 'kind of behaviours professionals look for' in diagnosing ASD. It recognises that there is 'no conclusive diagnostic test' and that 'it is quite common for professionals to disagree over the diagnosis given to a particular child' (ibid.: 2.9). No particular profession appears to have ultimate responsibility or intensive specialist training to diagnose ASD. In practice, 'paediatricians, psychiatrists, speech and language therapists, clinical or educational psychologists, or general practitioners (GPs) may contribute to a diagnosis of ASD' (ibid.). Guidelines for the diagnosis of autism should be developed by 'an independent, non-governmental, multi-disciplinary group of professionals' (ibid.: 2.10).

Despite these admitted difficulties of diagnosis and the need for guidelines, there still appears to be the potential to find still more children with ASD. The report states that it is 'difficult to know exactly how many children have ASD as it is not always easy to identify; indeed some will never have been diagnosed (ibid.: 2.16). Also, 'there is much to be done to improve awareness ... of the needs of ethnic minority children and their families. They are under-represented in terms of referrals for diagnosis' (ibid. 2.19). It is not clear whether this 'under-representation' implies that it would be advisable to seek to identify a proportionate percentage of children with ASD among various ethnic minority groups so that it cannot be claimed that discrimination is denying the 'right' of such minorities to be diagnosed as autistic.

It will be interesting to see if, in future years, there are further increases as 'identification' improves and whether this leads to calls for further training, better provision, national co-ordination, greater awareness and other requirements necessitating further resources. If all this is seen in the context that prevalence rates are unreliable because of inconsistency of diagnosis (Schreibman, 1988), then the possibility that this reflects, in part, economic interests being served in a redistributive society cannot be easily dismissed.

The importance of local agreements

In Chapter 3, the importance of developing local criteria for SEN was discussed. In the examples of dyslexia and autistic spectrum disorder discussed, here, if there is any concern that economic factors might be influencing the apparent increase in these conditions, this further underlines the importance of reaching local agreements on how such conditions will be identified, assessed and provided for. It is particularly important that local agreements are reached by LEA officers in partnership with schools, parents and others.

Thinking points

Practitioners may wish to consider:

- recommended approaches to funding; and
- the use of local agreements to protect against economic incentives that influence the identification of certain conditions.

Key text

Department for Education and Skills (DfES) (2001c) *The Distribution of Resources to Support Inclusion*. London, DfEE.
This publication sets out a recommended approach to SEN funding.

7

The Medical Model in an Integrated Approach

Introduction

This chapter introduces the main elements of a medical model of SEN, outlining the 'scientific' aspects of this approach and highlighting the importance of medical terminology. It considers criticisms of the model: it is insufficiently holistic; it gives too little consideration to patient participation; and it violates the rights of patients. The chapter examines a US approach to the classification of mental disorders which uses aspects of the medical model to identify learning difficulties and disabilities. It examines a possible postmodern alternative to the medical model and the implications this has for special education. Finally, it considers a possible synthesis of the medical and social models into a 'biopsychosocial' approach that identifies empirically the extent of medical and social influences in individual circumstances, thus allowing action to be taken accordingly.

What is the medical model?

Elements of the model

A 'model' is a social construct or framework in which one can examine society's understanding and interpretation of social behaviours (Cunningham and Davies, 1985). It has been claimed that a medical model is dominant in special education and that, no matter how some might wish otherwise, it 'still dominates the conceptualising of the problems students face in schools' (Booth, 1998: 84). It has also been suggested that in advanced western societies the dominant view of disability is medical, and people are regarded as disabled, 'as a result of their physiological or cognitive impairments' (Drake, 1996: 148). For Barnes and Mercer (1996), the medical model emphasises deficits and personal and functional limitations that are the responsibility of the person concerned. These functional limitations cause any disadvantage the person experiences and it is assumed these can be put right only by treatment or cure. The notions of individual loss and inability are seen as linked with the idea of dependency on society. In turn, such a dependency model (Campbell and Oliver, 1996) is considered to affect the identity of many disabled people.

In the *International Classification of Functioning, Disability and Health* (World Health Organisation, 2001: 20) the medical model is described as viewing disability 'as a problem of the person, directly caused by disease, trauma or other health condition, which requires medical care provided in the form of individual treatment by professionals'. Underlying the medical model is the view that there is a 'problem' or deficit, and it is generally assumed that this is predominantly within the patient. Bailey (1998) characterises the medical model as a professional orientation that focuses on:

- pathology and sickness;
- the nature of the aetiology (causal factors) and the presenting problem; and
- dealing with the problem.

This implies that the focus is not normalcy, wellbeing, the person with the problem or the social or ecosystem that surrounds the problem. Neither is, the centre of attention the patient, the patient's family nor social and financial circumstances; nor is the focus values and attitudes. The centre of attention is patient pathology.

In parallel with this is an approach to diagnosis that involves being able to recognise signs and symptoms, classifying these in terms of a condition, predicting from this the likely course of the disease or condition and finally offering intervention. Action to save a life or to prevent imminent threat from illness or disease is clearly an important part of the model. Later action may include preventive advice such as that relating to a healthy diet or stopping smoking. But the essential element is that pathology is identified and action taken to ameliorate the condition or to restore health.

Some implications of a 'scientific' approach

The medical model may be seen as an example of a scientific approach to SEN. Such an approach may come to regard the process of discovering objective truth as being predominantly about accumulating knowledge, without being sufficiently critical about the limitations of the process. Bhaskar (1986: 51) refers to 'the distinction between the (relatively) unchanging real objects which exist outside and perdue independently of the scientific process and the changing (and theoretically imbued) cognitive objects which are produced as a function and result of its practice'. In Bhaskar's view, the 'cognitive objects' that are produced as a function and result of the scientific process are changing and 'theoretically imbued'. In relation to the medical model, the language of diagnosis appears to translate supposedly objective phenomena into theoretically imbued 'objects'. As Bayliss (1998: 68) puts it, the language of diagnosis 'establishes the object, defines a programme of intervention and evaluates its outcome'.

The importance of medical terminology

The central role of the medical model is evident in the draft descriptions of SEN categories required by the DfES in connection with the Pupil Level Annual Schools Census (PLASC) from 2004 onwards. The DfES (as recommended by the Audit Commission) is asking for the pupils' greatest/primary and secondary needs. The DfES recognises that there is a wide spectrum of SEN and that many pupils have inter-related needs. But to aid planning and policy development, more information is required about the child's main need. The DfES has therefore adopted the broad categories already used by OfSTED:

- Specific learning difficulty (dyslexia, dyscalculia, dyspraxia).
- Moderate learning difficulty.
- Profound and multiple learning difficulty.
- Behavioural, emotional and social difficulty.
- Speech, language and communication need.
- Hearing impairment.
- Visual impairment.
- Multisensory impairment.
- Physical difficulty.
- Autistic spectrum disorder (including Asperger's syndrome).

The dominance of the medical model can be further illustrated by the difficulty of avoiding medical/deficit language without, at the same time, appearing to evade the existence of disabilities and difficulties. For example, I-CAN's *Joint Professional Framework* (2001), wherever possible, uses the term 'children with speech, language and communication needs' (SLCN). This document explains that this term avoids such words as 'difficulty', 'impairment', 'delay' and 'deviance', which 'tend to pathologise language acquisition' (ibid.: 3).

While the term SLCN does not suggest that the child 'does not have a problem', it indicates that the pupil's language is 'modifiable' and that there are 'possibilities of progress and change' (ibid.). Also, SLCN avoids assuming that 'the cause of the difficulty is solely within the child' and conveys that other people important to the child play crucial role in helping the child to overcome difficulties. Yet the problems of trying to avoid such terms are evident throughout the document. I-CAN's vision and goals relate to children with 'speech and language *impairments*'. The charity is described as being 'for children with speech and language *difficulties*' (ibid: 5, emphasis added). The foundation level of the framework is presented as concerning 'speech and language *difficulties*' (ibid.: 9) in one section and 'speech, language and communication *needs*' in another (ibid.: 15). Learning outcomes include evaluating 'the concept of specific language *impairment*' (ibid.: p.12). The glossary includes definitions of '*delay*', '*disorder*' and 'semantic-pragmatic *disorder/difficulty*' (emphasis added).

Criticisms of the medical model

It has been suggested that the medical model:

- is insufficiently holistic;
- is insufficiently concerned with patient participation; and
- violates patients' rights to be responded to as a person, not an object.

Insufficiently holistic

The medical model can appear reductionist and narrow, leading to patients being viewed in terms of their pathology. Care tends to be described in terms of physiology and disease and, therefore, the patient as a whole is overlooked and psychological and social factors are not taken sufficiently into account. Furthermore, research has suggested that more holistic approaches improve health care.

This view links the medical model with the attitudes of doctors who tend to see their patients in terms of their pathology. In one sense such attitudes are inevitable. To criticise a doctor for doing this is rather like criticising a lawyer for regarding his or her clients in terms of the legal situation they find themselves in. However, it would be unacceptable if lawyers conveyed to their client that their clients were of no interest to them as people, only as 'cases'. Similarly, most people would consider it inappropriate if doctors gave the impression that their patients are not, first and foremost, people but merely and exclusively pathologies. It is also possible to take into account psychological and social factors while still using the medical model. For example, once a patient has had an operation to reduce the likelihood of further strokes, the doctor may provide or recommend advice on changes in diet.

Insufficiently concerned with patient participation

It has been suggested that the medical model does not pay enough attention to the role of the patient in managing his or her medication, and that patients are made to feel too compliant. This suggests patients should be more responsible for their own health and should recognise that they have an impact on their own health (Chewning and Sleath, 1996).

There is, however, nothing in the medical model that precludes this. What may be problematic is if a doctor is authoritarian and takes insufficient notice of patients' concerns (for example about side-effects or other long-term effects of medication). This seems to be an issue about the doctor–patient relationship, not about the model.

Violating patient rights

Under medical model, the patient might be viewed more as an object than a person. The ability and potential of patients might be given insufficient attention, while the model itself promotes patient helplessness. However, this argument seems to be circular. Certain 'rights' appear to be invented when it is claimed that patient should not be viewed in the light of a model that treats them as objects. As the model is judged to treat patients as objects, patients 'rights' are therefore being violated. This issue again seems largely to concern the manner of the exchange between the doctor and patient rather than the model itself.

An important point, however, is the extent to which the model ignores patients' abilities and potential. In using the model, it is important that doctors retain an awareness of what patients can do. Again, however, the extent to which a patient feels helpless and lacking in power is likely to be related to the manner of the doctor–patient interaction. It can be argued that this is not inevitable within the intrinsic features of the model.

■ 'Mental disorders': classification and deficit views

It was suggested earlier that the medical model's approach to diagnosis involves being able to recognise signs and symptoms, classifying these in terms of a condition, predicting from this the likely course of the condition and finally offering intervention. An example of such an approach to mental disorders is the American *Diagnostic and Statistical Manual of Mental Disorders (4th edn)* (American Psychiatric Association, 1994), sometimes referred to as the DSM-IV. The editors of DSM-IV suggest that the need for the classification and categorisation of mental disorders 'has been clear throughout the history of medicine' (ibid.: xvi). The numerous nomenclatures of the past and present have differed in the degree of emphasis placed on defining such features as aetiology (the causal factors of conditions) and the course of the condition. They have also varied according to whether the main purpose was to use the categorisation in clinical, research or statistical settings.

It is accepted that categorisation is imperfect and that the notion of mental disorder 'lacks a consistent operational definition that covers all situations' (ibid.: xxi). Nevertheless, it has been considered useful to define mental disorders according to irrationality, disability, the pattern of a syndrome, aetiology and statistical deviation. It is not assumed that each category of mental disorder is completely discrete, with 'absolute' boundaries separating the disorder from other mental disorders or from an absence of mental disorder. All individuals with a mental disorder are not assumed to be the same as others with the same mental disorder in every important respect. In recognition of this, some conditions are described in terms of what the DSM-IV calls 'polythetic criteria sets', through which an individual can be diagnosed as having a condition even if all the symptoms listed are not present but only certain of them (DSM-IV. p. xxii).

The concept of mental disorder (despite the obvious fact that there is a mental element in many physical conditions and a physical element in many mental conditions), is considered useful in guiding decisions relating to conditions on the boundary between normal and pathological. The mental disorders included in the DSM-VI are associated with present distress, disability ('impairment in one or more important areas of functioning'), significantly increased risk of death, pain, disability or important loss of freedom (ibid.: xxi). The attempt at classification is not intended to categorise people but to classify the mental disorders they experience.

Those who worked on the DSM-IV rejected a dimensional model in favour of a categorical model. The dimensional model was considered to be best suited to factors that are distributed continuously in a population of people and that do not have clear boundaries (such as height). This model was thought to have limitations in that dimensional descriptions are less vivid and familiar than categories of mental disorder. There is also no agreement on the optimal dimensions to be used for the purposes of classification. However, the editors emphasise that clinical judgement is necessary in determining the use of categories and that the categories are not to be used mechanically.

The disorders specified in the DSM-IV that are most relevant to special education are listed below (NOS refers to 'not otherwise specified'):

- Mental retardation (mild, moderate, severe, profound, severity unspecified).
- Learning disorders (reading disorder [dyslexia], mathematics disorder, disorder of written expression, learning disorder NOS).

- Motor skills disorder (developmental co-ordination disorder).
- Communication disorders (expressive language disorder, mixed receptive-expressive language disorder, phonological disorder, stuttering, communication disorder NOS).
- Pervasive developmental disorders (autistic disorder, Rett's disorder, childhood disintegrative disorder, Asperger's syndrome, pervasive developmental disorder NOS).
- Attention deficit and disruptive behaviour disorders (attention deficit hyperactivity disorder, attention deficit hyperactivity disorder NOS, conduct disorder, oppositional defiant disorder, disruptive behaviour disorder NOS).
- Feeding and eating disorders in infancy or early childhood (pica, rumination disorder, feeding disorder of infancy or early childhood).
- Tic disorders (Tourette's disorder, chronic motor or vocal tic disorder, transient tic disorder, tic disorder NOS).
- Elimination disorders (encopresis, enuresis not due to medical condition).
- Other disorders of infancy, childhood or adolescence (separation anxiety disorder, selective mutism, reactive attachment disorder of infancy or early childhood, stereotypic movement disorder, disorders of infancy, childhood or adolescence NOS).

In the DSM-IV, the conditions are often described in terms of what the child cannot do – that is, in terms of deficits. For example, mental retardation is characterised by 'significantly sub-average intellectual functioning' as well as 'deficits or impairments' in adaptive functioning (ibid.: 37). Learning disorders are typified by academic functioning that is 'substantially below' what is expected, given the child's age, intelligence level and age-appropriate education. In motor skills disorders, skills are 'substantially below' similar expectations. Pervasive development disorders involve 'severe deficits and pervasive impairment' in many areas of development.

A postmodern alternative and its implications for special education

Some postmodern views offer a different understanding of disability and learning difficulty. Foucault provides a perspective that allows one to analyse the ways in which disabled identities are experienced and constructed. This perspective makes it possible for one to understand how the medical model identifies people with their pathologies. Foucault suggests that individuals are constructed as social objects who are knowable through disciplines and 'discourses'.

Formal and informal discourses construct individuals as subjects in two ways. They are subjects to others 'through control and restraint' and are subjects 'tied to their own identity by self knowledge' (Allen *et al.*, 1998: 26). Within the discourses are power/knowledge relationships and disciplinary techniques, such as the 'medical gaze' which acts to construct the patient. There are three mechanisms of surveillance within the 'gaze' (Foucault, 1977: 173): 'hierarchical observation', 'normalising judgements' and 'examinations'.

'Hierarchical observation' is seen by Foucault as a form of power which categorises the individual and imposes upon him or her a 'law of truth' which the individual has to recognise and which others have to recognise in the individual (Foucault, 1982: 212). In relation to special education, this might be interpreted as the intense surveillance that pupils with SEN are placed under by professionals and others. In SEN, the term 'normalising judgements' may be interpreted as the judgements made by professionals and others to determine which children have SEN and which do not. In some instances, being identified as having SEN can be seen as advantageous. Allen *et al.* (1998) suggest that this may relate to resources, saying that 'In a climate of resource constraints, distance from the norm has become valued'. This does not, however, explain why statements of SEN without resources attached to them are valued by some parents. One reason for this could be that the process of documentation indicates recognition that their child might have the condition that would begin to explain their difficulties. Also, even an unresourced statement of SEN gives some assurance that provision considered necessary will be made, and this is monitored through annual reviews and through the periodic evaluation associated with individual education plans.

'Examination' in Foucault's terms is considered to hold individuals in a 'mechanism of objectification' (1977: 187), and they may then be 'trained or corrected, classified, normalised, excluded' (ibid.: 191). In special education, one may ask to what extent this view characterises the multidisciplinary assessment that often leads to a statement of SEN.

Such a postmodern approach suggests that one should examine discourses and consider the way these might explain how the identities of children with SEN are constructed. This would include analysing such formal discourses as policies, statements of SEN, individual education plans and so on. It would also involve examining the day-to-day interactions of children with SEN and others, including teachers, other professionals, parents and other children.

Foucault indicates a method that may be used for analysing discourses. It has also been suggested that this method could be employed to analyse the official discourses on SEN and those that operate in schools (Allen, 1996). This method entails looking for evidence of 'individuals challenging their identities or opting for alternative experiences' (Allen *et al.* 1998: 28). The method might encourage teachers and others to move away from viewing individuals as having fixed identities or of being included or excluded. They might instead explore the 'oscillations within the pupils' discourses'. This would disturb the way in which disabled people are constructed as an undesirable part of such a dichotomy as able/disabled, ordinary/special. It would allow for the possibility of 'individual agency' and suggests the possibility of social change. Foulcault also recognises that, although power dominates, it allows opportunities for resistance because power is a relation and not a substance. When power is exchanged and circulated, there is always the possibility that relationships can be 'reversed, transformed and resisted' (Barker, 1998: 37).

Such an approach might appeal to anyone who views special education as being about the power and vested interests of professionals and who sees SEN as being about maintaining positions of power. But the concern to 'disturb' the way children with SEN are 'constructed' as the 'undesirable' part of an ordinary/special dichotomy may not be entirely productive. It could lead to the wishing away of disability (Cheu, 2002: 209): 'If you do not believe there is a disability, if you do not believe there is anything that needs to be "cured" or genetically prevented – that disability is indeed little more than a social construction – then you will likewise be freed from the need for cure.' One concern with such interpretations is that they could put at risk the financial and other support linked to disability and learning difficulty.

The medical model in identification, assessment and provision

If a postmodern alternative to the medical model can lead to a wishing away of disability and learning difficulties, a more credible approach is to try to integrate the medical model with an alternative – the social model. The *International Classification of Functioning, Disability and Health* (World Health Organisation, 2001: 3) (or ICF) aims to provide a common language and a shared framework for describing health and health-related matters. It defines the terms 'functioning' and 'disability' distinctively, and lists environmental factors that interact with these constructs:

- Functioning refers to all bodily functions.
- Disability refers to impairments (problems in body function or structure such as a significant deviation or loss), activity limitations and participation restrictions (ibid.: 3).

The ICF, which is not intended to be exclusively about disabled people but about all people, is organised in two parts. Part one concerns components of 'functioning and disability' and has two aspects:

1. The body (functions of body systems; body structures).
2. Activities and participation.

Part two is to do with components of 'contextual factors' and also has two aspects:

1. Environmental factors.
2. Personal factors.

The ICF does not intended to classify people, only to describe the situation of each individual within an 'array of health or health related domains' (ibid.: 8).

The medical model is depicted as viewing disability 'as a problem of the person, directly caused by disease, trauma or other health condition, which requires medical care provided in the form of individual treatment by professionals' (ibid.: 20). Medical care is the main issue and, politically, the principal response is to modify or reform health-care policy.

According to the ICF, the social model of disability sees the issue 'mainly as a socially created problem, and basically as a matter of the full integration of individuals into society' (ibid.: 20). Disability is a 'complex collection of conditions' (ibid.), many of them created by the social environment. The management of the problem requires social action. Society should be responsible for making the environmental modifications necessary so that people with disabilities can participate fully in all areas social life. The key issue is one of attitude or ideology that requires social change. Politically, this concerns human rights (ibid.).

The ICF regards these two models as opposing, and seeks to integrate them using a 'biopsychosocial approach'. This synthesis is intended to give 'a coherent view of different perspectives of health from a biological, individual and social perspective' (ibid. p. 20).

The ICF uses the term disability to denote 'multi-dimensional phenomena resulting from the interaction between people and their physical and social environment' (ibid.: 242). Disability is seen as a product of the 'interaction of the health characteristics and the contextual factors' (ibid.). Individuals should not be characterised exclusively in terms of their impairments, the activities that may be limited for them or restrictions to what they can participate in (ibid.). For example, rather than referring to a 'mentally handicapped person' the classification refers to a 'person with a problem in learning'.

It is suggested that the ICF can be useful in identifying where the principal problem of disability lies. This is considered to apply whether the problem is in the environment (in the sense of a barrier or the lack of a facilitator), whether it is related to the person's limited capacity or whether it is owing to a combination of factors (ibid.). If this is clarified, interventions can be targeted appropriately and their effects on levels of participation monitored and measured. In this way, objectives can be achieved that are 'concrete' and driven by evidence, and the 'overall goals of disability advocacy' can be furthered (ibid.).

Perhaps it is over-ambitious of the ICF to seek to integrate the contrasting social and medical models. The 'biopsychosocial approach' that ICF advocates is not, after all, a new model. It is a practical way of trying to give due weight to perceptions of a disability or learning difficulty that might be characterised as medical or social. This may still draw on different perspectives of health from a biological, psychological and social viewpoint but its application is, quite rightly, for the interpretation of real disabilities and learning difficulties. Such an approach seeks to draw on the strengths of the medical model while trying to combine this model with insights from other disciplines, such as psychology and sociology.

Thinking point

Practitioners may wish to consider the respective functions of the medical model and social approaches in empirically identifying influences in individual circumstances for children with learning difficulties and disabilities and responding accordingly.

◼ Key text

World Health Organisation (2001) *ICF – International Classification of Functioning, Disability and Health*. Geneva: WHO.

8

Sociological Influences in Special Education

Introduction

This chapter considers sociological influences on special education, in particular:

- functionalist and structural-functionalist approaches;
- conflict approaches;
- interpretative approaches;
- social constructionist and social creationist approaches; and
- 'adhocracy' and critical pragmatism.

It considers criticisms of social approaches to SEN. The chapter then examines current influences of sociological views of special education:

- Social elements in the *Special Educational Needs Code of Practice* (DfES, 2001a).
- The notion of 'barriers' to learning and participation.
- An interactionist approach, briefly reiterating the attempted synthesis of the social and medical models explained in Chapter 7.

Sociology and special education

Sociology, when applied to special education, endeavours to challenge what it sees as the 'recipe' approaches of psychology, medicine and unreflective pedagogy and offers broad perspectives that can lead to a fuller understanding of special education. It seeks to illuminate the social structures, social processes, policies and practices of special education and describes, analyses, explains and theorises about social interactions and relationships (Tomlinson, 1982). Applying the general principles and findings of sociology to the administration and processes of special education, the sociology of special education does three things:

1. It applies concepts such as society, culture, social class, community, status and role.
2. It compares the contexts in which special education takes place both within a particular society and between one society and another.
3. It analyses social processes within educational institutions.

Issues with which it is concerned include the effect of the economy on the sort of special education provided by the state and the social institutions (such as the family) involved in the process of special education. Other issues are the school as a formal organisation and social change in relation to special education.

Approaches in sociology

As various trends in sociology reflect different views of society, this section considers the following approaches:

■ Functionalist and structural-functionalist.
■ Conflict.
■ Interpretative.
■ Social constuctivist and social creationist.
■ 'adhocracy' and critical pragmatism.

Functionalist and structural-functionalist

A functionalist approach seeks to explain why social structures exist in relation to the part they play in society as a whole. It is a top-down theory, beginning with an analysis of society rather than of the individual. Important themes are the relationships between interdependent parts (e.g. the LEA, social services, health services, groups representing parents) and the way in which the functioning of the parts is vital for the wellbeing of society as a whole. People's values are considered to be the key determinants of their behaviour. The functionalist approach is based on the assumption that consensus in society is a normal state so that, while it is recognised that conflict does arise from time to time, this is explained as an evolutionary phenomenon.

In special education, a functionalist approach includes the use of such methods as the social survey, which aims to determine such 'facts' as the number of people with SEN. It may also see SEN as a 'social problem' and focus on organisation, management and provision in special education. A criticism is that this perspective, with its concentration on order and equilibrium, takes insufficient account of disorder and conflict. For example, a functionalist approach would have difficulty explaining the conflict that arises from time to time between those involved with SEN who may take different views: children, LEA officers, parents, teacher unions and so on (for a postmodern criticism of this approach, see Skrtic (1995a)).

A structural-functionalist explanation is also concerned with structure and equilibrium in society and is particularly associated with the work of Talcott Parsons (e.g. 1952). Structures in society are considered to interact with each other to perform positive roles for society as a whole so that every structure has some positive function. A weakness of such a view is that it is quite evident that some structures in society (such as organised crime) do not have a positive function. However, structures relating to the identification, assessment and provision for SEN would be likely to be considered as an example of structures with a positive function.

Accordingly, the approach is concerned with fitting children with SEN into society (for example, finding suitable employment for school leavers with SEN). The Warnock Report (DES, 1978) took a structural-functionalist view, presenting special education as a philanthropic response to children whose needs required special support.

Conflict

If functionalist and structural-functionalist views emphasise structure and equilibrium in society, conflict approaches look more to struggles between different groups and to vested interests (for example, those of professionals). These struggles are thought to centre round access to limited economic resources or power. Accordingly, conflict theories with a Marxist emphasis (given Marx's interest in analysing social conflict with reference to social class and the labour market) concentrated on class conflict about economic resources. Neo-Marxist conflict approaches in education regard a given educational structure as the result of social class struggles. Class interests lie behind any pattern of educational organisation, while economics is seen as a key determinant of behaviour.

Approaches relating to the work of Max Weber concentrated more on the struggle between different groups over power and status as well as resources. Weber argued that one group's dominance over another could arise in various ways, and that authority was an important aspect of dominance. In this view, group interests permeated education and dominant interest groups could reshape educational structures for their own ends (Weber, 1972).

Regarding special education, conflict approaches include considering historical development and the economic, political and social climates in which SEN developed. There is also a focus on the way such developments helped to maintain a particular order in society. A view of special education within a social world seen as characterised by conflict, domination and coercion is presented by Tomlinson (1982; 1995) and Sleeter (1995).

Interpretative approaches

An interpretative approach starts its analysis of society from the level of the individual and works 'up' to the level of society as a whole. Research tends to be focused upon small-scale interactions in everyday life. Interpretative orientations developed from perspectives that related to the social construction of the 'world' and the interactions of the participants in that world. Communication and interaction between people are considered to produce social categories and social knowledge. Reality is believed to be socially constructed (Berger and Luckmann, 1971).

In special education, the focus is on interactions such as those between a child with SEN and a teacher, for example, concentrating on how the child appears to be interpreting communications with the teacher and how these influence his or her views of him or herself and his or her environment (Ferguson and Ferguson, 1995) provide an example of an interpretative approach to special education).

Social constructivist and social creationist

A social constructionist perspective largely attributes the causes of disability to environmental factors. These include unsuitable teaching approaches and the negative attitudes of those who interact with the child. The perspective discourages labelling and categorisation, which are seen as a problem of individual medical/psychological approaches. The social constructionist view sees the 'problem' of perceived disability as being in the minds of able-bodied people, manifested in prejudice or social policies that reflect a 'tragic' view of disability. However, a difficulty with such a view is that there is a fine line between identifying difficulties, on the one hand, and of labelling on the other. A perspective that overemphasises social constructions of disability could damagingly make invisible those who may require support.

A social creationist perspective sees the 'problem' of perceived disability as being in the institutionalist practices of society. The creation of the notion of disability is seen as a form of oppression, and this oppression would be reduced if human difference or diversity were not just tolerated but celebrated. One aim is demanding changes in state and welfare provision to improve material conditions for disabled people (Allen *et al.*, 1998: 23). The approach has informed studies of knowledge and the curriculum, the classroom and teacher interactions (for example, it led to an adaptation model of classroom interaction – Woods (1979)).

'Adhocracy' and critical pragmatism

While not purely sociological, the views of Skrtic (1991; 1995b) regarding special education draw on social views of deviance and seem to suggest that

SEN, at least in part, is related to inappropriate and inflexible school organisation and an over-rigid professional culture and practices in mainstream teaching. He maintains that, in the twentieth century, a contradiction emerged between the ideal of universal education and the practicalities of schooling. Special education (separating children either within a mainstream or special school) developed to contain the failure of public education to provide for all children. Also, he sees special education as a response to pupil diversity within bureaucratic schooling. As such, in contrast to school bureaucracy, special education has emerged as an 'adhocracy' (associated with innovation, problem-solving, flexibility and inventing new programmes). This adhocracy indicates the structures and professional awareness that public education has to assume in order to prepare all future citizens to take part in democracy.

Skrtic uses 'critical pragmatism', derived from the philosophy of Dewey (1899/1976), as a method of investigating the presuppositions that have conditioned and limited professional discourse and practice. The method is used continuously to construct, 'deconstruct' and reconstruct educational practice and discourses. This requires that certain organisational conditions are present, and the adhocratic form that is typical of special education makes these conditions possible.

Some advocates of inclusion call for adhocratic values while wishing to retain professional bureaucracy and the organisational bureaucracy of schools. However, inclusion requires collaboration and mutual adjustment which are features of adhocracy, so reforms will require adhocratic school organisation and an adhocratic professional culture. While special education has been able to develop adhocratic values, the fact that it is separate does not allow for a dialogue to take place between mainstream and special educators, inhibiting any wider application of adhocratic professional practice. Consequently, practice develops bureaucratically and this reproduces the contradiction between bureaucracy, on the one hand, and education for all pupils on the other in the professional culture of special education.

Skrtic argues that, given its current professionally organised bureaucracy, public education cannot provide for all pupils. However, education can be for all if it adopts:

- adhocratic school organisation as the condition for critical practice; and
- critical pragmatism as a mode of professional discourse.

Skrtic's approach offers ways in which mainstream schools might be able to educate a more diverse population of pupils with SEN than they do presently. But it offers no indication of the practicalities that might be involved. Similarly, critical pragmatism may offer a method for reflective professional development but it gives no indication of what the content of this development would be.

General criticisms of social approaches

Several approaches to SEN have features in common, as well as differences. Functionalist and structural-functionalist explanations can be seen as supportive of a staus quo in which special education is accepted as providing for children 'needing' support and in which an element of within-child explanations of SEN would be acceptable. Conflict approaches suggest that there is much more to SEN than the apparent needs of children. Professional vested interests and other factors may influence the identification of children with SEN and the maintenance of special education as a social structure.

Social explanations are also to the fore in interpritative approaches, where SEN can be seen more as a social category produced by the interaction between people than as an objective phenomenon. Even more strongly, social constructivist and social creationist explanations push the understanding of SEN into the social rather than the within-child sphere. The use of adhocracy and critical pragmatism implies that, to a degree, the SEN of children are affected by over-rigid organisation and cultures in mainstream schools.

To varying degrees, then, particularly in conflict, interpretative, social constructivist and social creationist explanations, SEN is regarded as an outcome of social processes. In this light, special education can be seen as a response to socially produced SEN and informed more by power and vested interests than by a rational response to any real need.

A second thread in social approaches to SEN is the emphasis on values conveyed in such concepts as 'rights' and 'inclusion'. In conflict explanations, if special education is taken to be characterised by co-ercion and domination, it follows that this should be resisted and, instead, that 'rights' should be asserted that could counter such domination. Similarly, social constructivist approaches suggest a response that resists prejudice and supposed disabling social policies. Social creationist explanations call for the casting-off of oppresion by changing society so that diversity is celebrated and inclusion is seen as a 'right'.

Among cricisms of social approaches to SEN are that:

■ they may be insufficiently open to different approaches;
■ their view of oppression justifying inclusion lacks empirical derivation; and
■ they do not recognise sufficiently the dilemas associated with individual pupil differences.

Insufficient openness to different perspectives

It is not always easy constantly to be aware of the constraints and limitations of any one perspective in special education. Anyone with particular expertise and knowledge in any one perspective, even when he or she is aware of the criticisms of the perspective and possible responses to these criticisms, perhaps risks becoming insular. Sociologists are no exception. Kellman (1970: 94) has noted that social reasearch cannot be value free and that it is important for researchers to remain aware of the values brought to their own research and seek to take account of them in framing and carrying out research and in interpreting findings.

Even when one is aware of one's perspective there may be a resistance to evidence that is contrary to it. For example, Phtiaka (1998) takes the view that special schools segregate and that this is not necessarily beneficial. She gives an account of a study of 'deviant' pupils in a residential special school conducted by Cooper (1993). Phtiaka reports that Cooper (in looking into these special schools) discovered that the pupils found the experience both rewarding and personally 'enriching'. In this setting, the pupils experienced higher self-esteem and reported an improved sense of control over their own lives. Phtiaka's reaction to this information is not to consider that it might just conceivably be evidence contrary to her own perspective. She responds that the 'danger' of 'pupil rationalisation' needs to be kept in mind. Also, rewarding and enriching experiences are what these pupils 'should have been offered' in the mainstream schools (Phtiaka, 1998: 27).

Lack of empirical derivation for oppression as a justification for inclusion

Regarding inclusion, there is no empirical derivation of the belief that oppression is endemic within social institutions such as schools, or the view that 'equity' and 'inclusion' are desirable (Clark *et al.*, 1998). They are both accepted positions from which any analysis starts. Empirical inquiry takes on an illustrative role. Examples of oppression may be found, but the notion of oppression is a 'given'. No amount of evidence or inquiry would invalidate that position. The notion of inclusion is another given. It is sometimes said, therefore, that this approach is based on ideal types and idealised models rather than real life in schools (Lingard, 1996).

Dilemmas of individual differences

The social approach avoids categorising pupils. It recognises difference but sees this as existing at the individual level. The development of categories is seen as likely to ignore the complexity of individuals and may lead to responses to those individuals that are arbitary or even oppressive. More authentic resposes to individual differences are therefore ad hoc. Consequently, it is practically impossible to develop an explanatory theory of human difference or to accumulate and formalise pedagogical knowledge if that knowledge is based on responses to 'stable dimensions of difference between learners' (Clarke *et al.*, 1998: 166).

Such socially informed pedagogical approaches as there have been, focus on problem-solving, adhocracy and mechanistic models of the curriculum. From these it is expected that the structures and practices that will deliver equity and inclusion will emerge. This seems to miss the point that, once a curriculum has been determined, it will lead inevitably to some children learning within it better than others. Pupil differences persist, whether or not one constructs categories.

Sociological influences in special education guidance and perspectives

So far this chapter has outlined several sociological approaches and has suggested specific criticisms of these, as well as broader criticisms of sociological approaches to SEN in general. However, the ways in which social approaches have influenced special education are evident in some aspects of special education guidance and elswhere. This section therefore considers:

■ social elements of the *Special Educational Needs Code of Practice* (DfES, 2001a);
■ the notion of 'barriers' to learning; and
■ the contribution of social perspectives to interactive approaches to SEN.

Social elements of the *Special Educational Needs Code of Practice*

The *Special Educational Needs Code of Practice* (DfES, 2001a) presents an interactive view of learning and SEN that involves social and 'within child' factors. Within this perspective, social elements are naturally evident. In considering identification, assessment and provision in the primary phase, the code states that assessment should always be 'fourfold', focusing on (ibid.: code 5.6):

■ the child's learning characteristics;
■ the learning environment the school is providing for the child;
■ the task; and
■ the teaching style.

If one were to focus too much on the child's 'learning characteristics', this could lead to view of learning that overemphasises within-child difficulties. It is also important, therefore, to take account of the 'learning environment'. The task and the teaching style can perhaps be regarded as being intermediaries between any difficulties in learning the child may have and the learning environment provided by the school.

It is stated that 'some difficulties in learning may be caused or exacerbated by the school's learning environment or adult/child relationships'. The code suggests looking at certain matters to decide how these can be developed so the child can learn effectively. These 'matters' include (ibid.):

- classroom organisation;
- teaching materials;
- teaching style; and
- differentiation.

If it is assumed that the code is using the term 'difficulties in learning' in its legal sense, it does not follow that the pupils to which it refers in the passage quoted will have SEN. They may have difficulties in learning that are not 'significantly greater' than the majority of children of the same age in terms of s. 312 of the Education Act 1996. However, the code still recognises that environmental factors are important in the learning of children whose 'difficulties in learning', if not sufficiently addressed, may become more significant – perhaps leading to learning difficulties and SEN.

The chapter of the code dealing with 'Identification, assessment and provision in the secondary sector' relates environmental factors more directly to SEN, stating: 'Effective management, school ethos and the learning environment, curricular, disciplinary and pastoral arrangement can help prevent some special educational needs arising and minimise others' (ibid.: 6.18). Here it is clear that the code is speaking of SEN, and social factors such as 'ethos' and 'learning environment' are taken into account. To reinforce the point that one cannot assume within-child explanations of SEN, the code also states: 'Schools should not assume that pupils' learning difficulties always result solely, or even mainly, from problems within the young person' (ibid.).

If assessment involves environmental elements, and explanations of SEN take account of social explanations, then environmental aspects are also important in provision. When discussing the statutory assessment of SEN, refering to (among others) pupils who 'demonstrate features of emotional and behavioural difficulties', the code indicates that they may require the provision of 'a safe and supportive environment' (ibid.: 7.60).

Barriers to learning

The notion of barriers to learning may indicate a view of SEN that emphasises social influences rather than within-child factors. This is not always so and the term 'barriers' is sometimes used to refer to the child's difficulties themselves. For example, a chapter of the *Special Educational Needs Code of Practice* (DfES, 2001a) concerning early education settings considers 'triggers' for referral for seeking help from outside agencies. These include that, despite receiving an individualised programme and/or concentrated support, the child 'has ongoing communication or interaction difficulties that impede the development of social relationship and cause substantial barriers to learning' (ibid.: 4.31). In the quotation above, it appears that the child's 'difficulties' not only impede development but 'cause' substantial barriers. However, the expression 'barriers' usually refers to a more social perspective of SEN in which it is believed that, if the barriers are removed or minimised, the SEN will be removed or reduced. It appears to be in this sense that the term is used in National Curriculum documents (QCA/DfEE, 1999a; 1999b). One of the three principles of inclusion is the overcoming of potential barriers to learning and assessment for individuals and groups of pupils. The National Curriculum documents make clear that it refers to pupils with SEN (as well as others). The *Handbook* for primary teachers states: 'A minority of pupils will have particular learning and assessment requirements which ... if not addressed, could create barriers to learning. These requirements are likely to arise as a consequence of a pupil having special educational need or disability' (QCA/DfEE, 1999a: 33). Here the emphasis is on 'requirements' relating to learning and assessment that need to be addressed so that they do not 'create' barriers to learning. However, the interactive nature of SEN seems to be recognised in the specific guidance relating to SEN, which indicates that curriculum planning and assessment for pupils with SEN must take into account the 'type and extent of the difficulty experienced by the pupil' (ibid.).

In the guidance, *Inclusive Schooling: Children with Special Educational Needs* (DfES, 2001e: 2), one of the principles of an inclusive education service is that schools, LEAs and others 'should actively seek to remove barriers to learning and participation'. In developing effective inclusion, schools (supported by LEAs and others) 'should actively seek to remove the barriers to learning and participation that can hinder or exclude pupils with special educational needs' (ibid.).

In a more general sense, social views can explain some aspects of physical disability in terms of social 'barriers' to participation, such as a lack of ramps for wheelchairs and other forms of physical access. Barriers are also seen in terms of the negative attitudes and expectations of others. It is perhaps in this sense that one might consider that there could be barriers to learning for children with profound and multiple learning difficulties brought about by brain injury. However, with reference to such severe learning difficulties, within-child perspectives appear more convincing. Accordingly, it has been argued that the social model 'has failed to include all aspects of disability, has focused on people with physical disabilities, and has marginalised people with intellectual disabilities' (MacKay, 2002: 161; see also Chappell, 1998; Humphrey, 2000).

Interactive approaches

Interactive approaches regard the environment as an interactive structure, while individuals are seen as 'active synthesisers of information from the environment' (Llewellyn and Hogan, 2000: 161; see also Crow, 1996). In an interactive outlook, several dimensions are taken into account together. Chapter 7 described an attempt to synthesise the medical and social model, and this will be very briefly reiterated here. The *International Classification of Functioning, Disability and Health* (World Health Organisation, 2001) (or ICF) summarises the main differences between the medical and social models.

The ICF regards the medical model as viewing disability 'as a problem of the person, directly caused by disease, trauma or other health condition, which requires medical care provided in the form of individual treatment by professionals' (ibid.: 20). Medical care is the main issue and, politically, the principal response is to modify or reform health-care policy. The social model sees the issue 'mainly as a socially created problem, and basically as a matter of the full integration of individuals into society' (ibid.). Disability is a complex collection of conditions, many of them created by the social environment. The management of the problem requires social action. Society should be responsible for making the environmental modifications necessary so that people with disabilities can take part fully in all aspects of social life. The key issue is to do with negative attitudes or ideologies, and changing these is considered to require social change. Politically, this concerns human rights (ibid.).

The ICF seeks to integrate the models through a 'biopsychosocial approach' that intends to give a cohesive picture of different perspectives of health from a 'biological, individual and social perspective' (ibid.). Within its interactive view, the ICF sees disability as 'multi-dimensional phenomena resulting from the interaction between people and their physical and social environment' and as a product of the 'interaction of the health characteristics and the contextual factors' (ibid.: 242).

The ICF can be useful in identifying where the principal 'problem' of disability lies, 'whether it is in the environment by way of a barrier or the absence of a facilitator, the limited capacity of the individual himself or herself, or some combination of factors' (ibid.). If this is clarified, interventions can be targeted better and their effects on inclusion monitored and measured. It will be seen that, in such interactive approaches, social perspectives make an important contribution.

Thinking points

Practitioners may wish to consider further the influence of sociological perspectives in other documents, such as:

■ *Excellence for All Children: Meeting Special Educational Needs* (DfEE, 1997a); and
■ current documents published by voluntary and charitable organisations.

Key text

Shakespeare, T. (ed.) (1998) *The Disability Reader: Social Science Perspectives*. London: Cassell. Particularly the chapter by A.L. Chappell, 'Still out in the cold: people with learning difficulties and the social model of disability'.

9

Psychological and other Approaches to Teaching and Learning

Introduction

This chapter considers approaches to teaching and learning developed within a psychological framework: behavioural and cognitive-behavioural techniques and approaches derived from Piaget's theory of development and learning. Emotional intelligence is briefly described. The chapter considers approaches to teaching and learning associated with the Office for Standards in Education (2003a; 2003b; 2003c; 2003d) and Hay McBer (2000). The *National Special Educational Needs Specialist Standards* (TTA, 1999) are outlined. It is important that methods are developed in the case of all these approaches to ensure they are practicable with whole classes while, at the same time, addressing the learning needs of individual pupils with SEN. With this in mind, the chapter outlines the approaches to teaching in three government strategies:

- The National Literacy Strategy (DfEE, 1998a).
- The National Numeracy Strategy (DfEE, 1999a).
- The Key Stage 3 strategy in relation to developing literacy and numeracy across the curriculum (DfEE, 2001a; 2001b).

The chapter concentrates on organisational aspects of providing for the learning needs of diverse pupil populations. These may be used in balancing whole-class teaching and individual and small-group work for pupils with SEN. The contribution of learning support assistants is considered.

Psychological approaches to teaching and learning

Particularly influential among psychological approaches to teaching and learning are well established behavioural and cognitive-behavioural perspectives and approaches derived from Piaget's theory of development and learning.

Behavioural

Behaviourally orientated methods have included task analysis (Howell *et al.*, 1979), direct instruction (Carnine and Silbert, 1979) and precision teaching (Raybould and Solity, 1998). A familiar and substantiated approach to early education using behavioural principles is the Portage programme (White and Cameron, 1987), while the long-standing Education of the Developmentally Young Programme (Foxten and McBrien, 1981; McBrien *et al.*, 1992) is similarly based on behavioural methods.

A behavioural approach characterised as 'assessment through teaching' involves determining a sequence for the curriculum the child is to follow, placing the child on the curriculum sequence, deciding what to teach, selecting the appropriate teaching methods and arrangements, and assessing the pupil's progress (Solity and Raybould, 1988).

Such strategies have particular strengths where specific behaviour and skills are concerned, both in seeking to explain how the behaviour develops and in modifying it. But these approaches tend to be less successful in aspects of education that do not lend themselves so easily to behavioural explanations, such as acquiring knowledge and ways of thinking. Both these aspects seem better explained and developed by cognitive-behavioural approaches and by methods that take due regard of social aspects of education.

Cognitive-behavioural

Dockerell and McShane's (1993) cognitive-behavioural approach involves addressing a difficulty in learning something (or 'problem manifestation') by taking account of the child, the task he or she is required to carry out and his or her environment. The 'problem manifestation' therefore suggests the appropriate level of intervention. This intervention is also informed by variables relating to:

■ the child (such as what the child already knows);
■ the task (for example, the type of task and its level); and
■ the environment (for example, classroom organisation and the involvement of parents).

An approach emphasising the interaction between the learner and others is the model proposed by Gallimore and Tharpe (1990), drawing on the work of Vygotsky. Put very briefly, Vigotsky regarded all speech as essentially social. He viewed individual learning as the internalised consequences of social activity mediated through speech or another sign system (Vygotsky, 1987). Through tutoring, the child is provided with a context for learning. As the task becomes increasingly familiar to the child, the tutor leaves more for the child to do unaided until the child can perform the whole task successfully. A mature learner reflects this social form of learning by, in a sense, instructing him or herself when faced with new or difficult tasks.

Vygotsky proposed a zone of proximal development (ZPD), which is the distance between the learner's actual development level (judged by independent problem-solving) and the potential development, determined by problem-solving in collaboration with an adult or more capable peers (Vygotsky, 1978). His ZPD offers an explanation of how learning can progress with varying degrees of support. At the same time, it indicates a way in which learning can be enhanced and increased. It may apply to pupils with SEN as well as to pupils not identified as having SEN as the level or type of learning is unspecified.

Lave and Wenger (1991: 48) having suggested that operational definitions of the ZPD have been interpreted in several ways, identifying 'scaffolding', 'cultural' and 'societal' interpretations. The 'scaffolding' interpretation distinguishes between the support given to the learner in the initial performance of the tasks and later performance without such support. Gallimore and Tharpe (1990) developed a four-stage model of performance capacity in which the first two stages taken together have similarities with the 'scaffolding' interpretation of Vygotsky's ZPD. In Gallimore and Tharpe's stage 1, others who are more capable provide assistance for the learner. In their stage 2, the learner him or herself provides the assistance. In other words, progress is seen as a move from social control to self-control.

An advantage of such cognitive approaches is that, being less structured than some of the behavioural methods, they allow more uncertainty and unpredictability and, consequently, a greater likelihood of arriving at unexpected but desirable learning outcomes. Pupils appear to learn interpersonal skills more effectively, and cognitive approaches help pupils generalise and try different ways of applying their knowledge (Smith and Cowrie, 1991). A key feature of such methods is the social interaction between the learner and the teacher in which both participants modify their understanding of each other's activity as they seek the way forward in learning.

Piaget's theory of development and learning

Piaget viewed intelligence as a process that changes over time and as the means by which individuals adapt to their environment. It involves the individual attempting to construct an understanding of reality through his or her interaction with it (Piaget and Inhelder, 1969; Piaget 1970). An important feature of Piaget's theory is the 'schema': a unit of intelligent behaviour enabling experience to be organised to make the environment more predictable. Schemas include actions and skills, ideas, aspects of knowledge and verbal labels.

Developmental changes are thought to be underpinned by the functions of 'assimilation', 'accommodation' and 'equilibrium'. 'Assimilation' involves the child taking in new experiences and fitting them into existing schema. 'Accommodation' is the process through which the child adjusts an existing schema to fit in with the environment. 'Equilibrium' (balance with the environment) is a state for which the child strives through adaptation. It is achieved through the complementary processes of assimilation and accommodation. Piaget proposed a continuous, progressive process of cognitive development summarised as stages, each of which represented characteristic schemas and changes. These stages are as follows:

■ Sensori-motor (0–2 years). The child progresses from being focused on immediate sensory and motor experiences to having a basic capacity for thinking.
■ Preoperational (2–7 years) comprising preconceptual (2–4 years) and intuitive (4–7 years). The preconceptual period builds on the child's capacity for symbolic thought. In the intuitive period, the child begins more systematically to develop the mental operations of ordering, quantifying and classifying.
■ Concrete operational (7–11 years). The child is able to reason in terms of objects (for example, the relations between objects when the objects are physically present).
■ formal operational (11–15 years). The child is able to reason hypothetically.

The ages for each stage were approximations and children were thought to move through these stages at different rates (for example, because of environmental factors). However, the sequence of stages was considered to be invariant and universal and to relate to biological maturation.

Several studies have indicated that, in the sensory motor stage, children demonstrate concepts and abilities earlier than Piaget thought (e.g. Baillargeon and DeVos, 1991; Meltzoff and Moore, 1994). In the preoperational stage, Piaget found that children have difficulty making certain inferences involving an experiment using rods of different lengths. But it has been demonstrated (Bryant and Trabasso, 1971) that children could sometimes perform the inference task if first trained in a way that ensured they could remember what was asked of them. While Piaget's observations of the concrete operational stage have been broadly confirmed (e.g. Tomlinson-Keasey, 1978), the development of the formal operational stage appears less predictable than Piaget thought (e.g. Shayer *et al.*, 1976; Shayer and Wylam, 1978).

According to Piaget's theory, strictly, it would not be possible deliberately to speed up the child's rate of development through interventions. The child's present level of cognitive functioning is considered to limit learning. Therefore instruction would be expected to produce only limited and perhaps temporary progress. However, others (e.g. Meadows, 1988) have indicated that training does significantly enhance performance. Both self-discovery learning and tutorial learning do so.

An approach to teaching and learning drawing on Piaget's theory involves the teacher judging the child's present stage of cognitive development and setting tasks framed to the 'needs' of the stage, which are therefore intrinsically motivating. The teacher provides the child with learning opportunities enabling progress to the next developmental step. Disequalibrium is created which leads to accommodation and equilibrium. The teacher seeks a balance between guiding the child's thinking patterns and setting up opportunities for the child to explore unaided (Thomas, 1985).

The teacher encourages the child (through active learning) to question, explore and experiment, and he or she seeks to understand the reasoning underlying the child's responses. The teacher encourages children to learn from one another and to hear other views. The curriculum is adjusted to each child's individual cognitive 'needs' and level (Smith and Cowrie, 1991) and may be reviewed in the light of Piagetian stages without being too constrained by them. When teaching pupils with SEN, practitioners should not assume that these stages cannot be expedited through teaching. Understanding the typical characteristics of each stage assists in consolidating learning and helping the child to progress, so long as it is informed by observation of what the child does and is not distorted by theoretical expectations.

Emotional intelligence

Emotional intelligence has been defined (Salovey and Sluyter, 1997: 10) as involving the ability to:

- perceive accurately, appraise and express emotion;
- access and/or generate feelings when they facilitate thought;
- understand emotion and emotional knowledge; and
- regulate emotions and promote emotional and intellectual growth.

A related model of emotional intelligence ranges in complexity from branch one ('perception, appraisal and expression of emotion') to branch four ('reflective regulation of emotions to promote emotional and intellectual growth'). Within each branch there is a progression in four levels. For example, branch three ('understanding and analysing emotions: employing emotional knowledge') progresses from level 1 (the ability to 'label emotions and recognise relations among the words and the emotions themselves') to level 4 (the ability 'to recognise likely transitions among emotions').

An important feature of emotional intelligence is the inter-relationship between emotions and the more traditional understanding of intelligence.

Office for Standards in Education approach

Another approach to teaching and learning is that of the Office for Standards in Education (OfSTED), implicit in the handbooks used by inspectors when inspecting schools and by schools when working on their own professional development and school improvement. An example of this is the assessment of quality of teaching in primary schools (OfSTED, 2003b). In determining judgements about how well pupils are taught, inspectors have to consider the extent to which teachers demonstrate certain skills. These are as follows:

- Showing good subject knowledge and understanding in the way they present and discuss their subject.
- Being technically competent in teaching basic skills such as phonetics.
- Planning effectively, setting clear objectives that pupils understand.
- Challenging and inspiring pupils, expecting the most of them so as to deepen their knowledge and understanding.
- Using methods that enable pupils to learn effectively.
- Managing pupils well and insisting on high standards of behaviour;
- Using time, support staff and other resources effectively.
- Assessing pupils' work thoroughly and using assessments to help pupils overcome difficulties.
- Using homework effectively to reinforce and/or extend what is learnt in school.

The Hay McBer perspective

Several structures exist to help one judge the quality of teaching provided for pupils, including those with SEN. Among these is the approach developed by Hay McBer (2000). Three factors within the teacher's control significantly affect pupils' progress:

1. Teaching skills.
2. Professional characteristics.
3. Classroom climate.

Teaching skills include such behaviours as involving all pupils in the lesson, differentiating work effectively and using different teaching methods, activities and techniques of questioning. Professional characteristics are patterns of behaviour that combine to drive teachers' practice. Classroom climate is a measure of the collective perceptions of pupils in relation to those dimensions of the classroom that directly impact on pupils' capacity and motivation to learn.

Outstanding teachers in primary and secondary schools scored highly on having high expectations. In primary schools, exceptional teachers had very good time and resource management skills. In secondary schools, exceptional teachers planned and managed homework well. Pupils in the classes of exceptional teachers were clear about what they were doing and why. They could recognise links to earlier learning. Pupils felt secure and found work both interesting and challenging. Work was suitably differentiated and teachers managed pupils well, providing clear boundaries for behaviour. Time and resource management was good, and more than 90% of pupils were focused on their tasks.

Exemplary teachers used a variety of assessment techniques, looking for improvement in knowledge and skills as well as gaps in understanding. They encouraged pupils to judge their work and to set targets. Homework was integrated into class work.

The research identified five sets of characteristics:

1. *Professionalism*: challenge and support, confidence, creating trust, respect for others.
2. *Thinking*: analytical and conceptual thinking.
3. *Planning and setting expectations*: drive for improvement, information seeking, initiative.
4. *Leading*: flexibility, holding people accountable, managing pupils, passion for learning.
5. *Relating to others*: impact and influence, teamworking, understanding others.

Outstanding teachers are able consistently to enthuse pupils and to achieve their full involvement. They create a positive atmosphere to secure the results planned. They provide a stimulating classroom environment giving demonstrations, checking understanding and giving practice at the level of the whole class, groups and individuals in using and applying skills and knowledge.

National Special Educational Needs Specialist Standards

The *National Special Educational Needs Specialist Standards* (TTA, 1999) refer to pupils with severe and/or complex SEN. The standards are intended as an audit tool to help teachers and headteachers identify training and development needs relating to teaching pupils with severe and/or complex SEN effectively. Teachers in mainstream schools, pupil referral units, special classes and mainstream school units, and staff in support and advisory services, may use them. Teachers in mainstream schools can focus on standards that support their developing role because of the expected increasing inclusion of pupils with SEN in mainstream schools. Headteachers in mainstream schools can use the standards to prepare for increased inclusion, perhaps auditing current expertise and establishing the school's priorities for specialist training and development of staff, and to inform the job descriptions of new staff.

The standards are applicable to teachers and managers in special classes and units in mainstream schools or pupil referral units. These staff may acquire further SEN expertise, perhaps by concentrating on the standards that help them meet the needs of pupils with more severe and complex SEN so that they can help teaching colleagues, learning support assistants and parents. The standards may apply to teachers and managers of support services. They can concentrate on the standards that to help them identify knowledge, understanding and skills that will help schools towards an increasing inclusion of pupils with SEN in mainstream. The aim would be to improve access to the curriculum, to help teachers differentiate teaching and learning better or to support schools and parents to make stronger links between school and home-based learning (ibid.: 1).

The standards can help schools and other training providers to develop, co-ordinate and improve existing training. Schools and others can also use the standards to promote continuing professional development and research to extend and improve inclusive practice. The SEN specialist standards cover core standards; extension standards; standards in relation to key SEN specialist roles and responsibilities; and skills and attributes.

The core standards form a starting point for the development of further expertise. They involve the following:

- Strategic direction and development of SEN provision nationally and regionally.
- Identification, assessment and planning.
- Effective teaching.
- Development of communication, literacy and numeracy skills and information and communications technology capability.
- The promotion of social and emotional development, positive behaviour and the preparation for adulthood (ibid.: 4).

Extension standards are intended to give a secure foundation for improving the education of pupils with the most severe and/or complex forms of SEN. They comprise communication and interaction; cognition and learning; behavioural, emotional and social development; and sensory and physical development. Under each of these headings are listed the specific knowledge, understanding and skills required by teachers of pupils who have autistic spectrum disorder, are deaf-blind or who have hearing or visual impairment.

Key SEN specialist roles and responsibilities are set out in standards relating to advisory, curricular and managerial roles and responsibilities. Skills and attributes summarise what is required to ensure optimum pupil progress. Particularly relevant is the section under core standards covering 'effective teaching, ensuring maximum access to the curriculum', which sets out what teachers with specialist knowledge, understanding and skills in the area will demonstrate. This includes, for example, analysing complex learning sequences and setting small achievable targets for pupils who require them. The teacher should be able to 'identify individual learning outcomes and develop, implement and evaluate a range of approaches'.

These approaches might include task analysis, skills analysis and target setting to help pupils achieve learning outcomes in various settings. Other skills comprise 'sequencing and structuring learning experiences and the learning environment' (ibid.: 11), adapting and modifying resources, using and evaluating specialist resources, and working with others to use effectively specialist environments such as sensory rooms (ibid.).

The National Literacy and Numeracy Strategies

General comments

A difficulty arises in the classroom when applying teaching and learning approaches such as those described in this chapter. The teacher in the busy modern classroom has to plan carefully to apply insights from these approaches to pupils with SEN to ensure that broad curriculum requirements are linked to individual circumstances. It is important that these issues are developed in the education and training of teachers at all stages.

There are implications for the role of the staff development co-ordinator and the SENCO. Initial teacher training and professional development need to address the issues of applying effective teaching models while providing for the individual learning needs of pupils with SEN. Aids to finding the right balance between whole-class teaching and individualised approaches are the National Literacy Strategy (NLS) and National Numeracy Strategy (NNS).

Both the literacy hour and the numeracy session have been vehicles for the development of approaches that provide opportunities for work with individual or small groups of pupils within a context of predominantly whole-class teaching. Where teachers give attention flexibly to different groups, this can help provide appropriately for many pupils with SEN. However, as the NNS guidance recognises, at some points it may be necessary to provide for pupils on individual programmes, perhaps supported by a learning support assistant.

Differentiation to create opportunities for individual work may involve setting work at different levels for different pupils, planning for different learning outcomes, offering different levels of support, employing resources to structure and support learning, and the judicious use of information and communication technology.

The National Literacy Strategy and SEN

Under the NLS framework, primary-phase classes are taught literacy each day for one hour of dedicated time. Work includes class-shared reading and writing and group-guided reading and writing, and the teaching of phonics, vocabulary, spelling, handwriting and grammar. About 40 minutes is spent in whole-class teaching and about 20 minutes in independent working.

The methodology of the 'literacy hour' encourages direct teaching and emphasises interaction between teachers and learners. Among the teaching strategies considered suitable (DfEE, 1998a) are:

- direction;
- demonstration;
- discussion;
- modelling (e.g. through shared reading);
- scaffolding (e.g. using writing frames);
- explanation;
- questioning;
- listening and responding;
- initiating and guiding exploration; and
- investigating ideas.

Within the NLS, the *Framework for Teaching* (DfEE, 1998a) sets out the aims of the NLS and offers guidance on the structure within which teaching should take place – the 'literacy hour'. DfEE guidance following the framework set out other approaches relevant to pupils with SEN:

- Different teaching strategies.
- Work set at different levels.
- Variations in the pace at which work is presented.
- Access to alternative communication systems, including signing, symbols, Braille and electronic devices.
- Parallel groups.

For some pupils, the Reading Recovery method is used to address 'the specific reading difficulties of those who, in spite of being taught well, fall behind' (Literacy Task Force/DfEE, 1997: 14). Also there were a remaining 5% of pupils each of whom needs an individual learning plan to meet his or her literacy needs (ibid.). Within the literacy hour, teachers therefore have to balance teaching literacy in a structured way and developing the flexibility to address pupils' particular literacy difficulties. The NLS has also been adapted for pupils in special schools (Berger *et al.*, 1999).

The NLS document suggests that many mainstream children with SEN will be able to achieve at the age-appropriate level in the NLS, given help and encouragement. Most are expected to benefit significantly from being involved in class work with their peers. Even where children with SEN need to work on different objectives, they should be taught with their own class and year group.

Among the ways of encouraging the inclusion of pupils with SEN in the literacy hour in ordinary schools are the teacher asking different pupils questions of different levels of complexity (DfEE, 1998a) and a teaching assistant providing support. Other advice is that manual signing or other appropriate systems of communication are used, and that special or adapted materials are employed (ibid.). Also, during the independent work section of the literacy hour, groups of pupils can work on 'catch-up' programmes and reading schemes in which work is focused on NLS framework objectives (preferably linked to the main class topic themes and teacher focus) (Gross *et al.*, 1999).

Some pupils with SEN may need to work outside the literacy hour while other pupils are working in the literacy hour session (for example, when extra support provided outside the literacy hour times or within it proves insufficient) (DfEE, 1998a: 115). Outside the literacy hour, pupils with SEN may benefit from additional approaches. These include cross-age peer tutoring and family literacy with parents and pupils working together. Another strategy is foundation building-work relating to objectives from earlier NLS levels or from a different key stage although to some extent, this may be accommodated within the literacy hour.

Recent research on particular interventions (Brooks, 2002) considers the effectiveness of evaluated intervention schemes that have been used in the UK. These are intended to improve the reading, spelling or writing attainment of lower-achieving pupils in at least one of the Years 1–6. The report suggests that it is often reasonable to expect substantial rates of progress and that several schemes have provided evidence of such an impact in at least one study. These include, for example, Reading Recovery, Phono-Graphics and paired reading.

The NLS implies three 'waves' of support, which can be related to the graduated response outlined in the *Special Educational Needs Code of Practice* (DfES, 2001a). Wave one concerns the inclusion of all pupils in an effective literacy hour. Pupils with SEN who are included are likely to be identified as requiring support in terms of School Action or School Action Plus. Wave two refers to small-group intervention, such as early literacy support (for Year 1), additional literacy support (Years 3 and 4), further literacy support (Year 5), booster classes and other interventions. These are intended to help pupils *not* having SEN related directly to learning difficulties in literacy or mathematics to catch up with peers. Where pupils in wave-two interventions are receiving support in terms of School Action or School Action Plus or have a statement of SEN, this may relate to such SEN as emotional and behavioural difficulties, communication and interaction difficulties or sensory or physical impairment.

Wave-three interventions are specifically for pupils with SEN. These pupils may have SEN relating to literacy or to other barriers to learning, and these pupils invariably receive support in terms of School Action or School Action Plus.

The National Numeracy Strategy and SEN

The NNS involves a structured daily mathematics lesson of 45 minutes to one hour for all primary-age pupils. Teachers teach the whole class together for a high proportion of the time, with oral and mental work being an important feature of each lesson. A typical lesson might include a session of oral work and mental calculation followed by the main teaching activity, and might conclude with a plenary session. Teachers whose classes include pupils with learning difficulties in mathematics can use the framework to identify suitable objectives to be incorporated into individual education plans, tracking back to earlier stages if appropriate. Pupils with severe or complex difficulties may need to be supported with an individualised programme.

Regarding the NNS in primary schools in England, several suggestions were made for pupils with SEN (DfEE, 1999a). These included the advice that teachers should 'plan some questions specifically for pupils ... with SEN, and ask named children to respond' (ibid.: 21). Where pupil's difficulties concern mathematics, it is suggested that teachers 'use the Framework to identify suitable objectives to be incorporated into individual education plans, tracking back to earlier stages if it is appropriate to do so' (ibid.: 23). It was suggested that pupils with hearing impairments may need to sit closer to the teacher or may need 'to be helped to take part in the activity through signing or support given by another adult' (ibid.: 21). These pupils could be 'introduced to the new vocabulary they will meet in next week's oral work' (ibid.: 22).

Pupils with physical or sensory disabilities were not expected to have to work on a separate programme. Only such adaptations may be needed as 'preparation for the oral and mental part of the lesson and the pace at which it is conducted, the use of signing, Braille and symbols, and the provision of a range of tactile materials, technological aids and adapted measuring equipment' (ibid.: 23). For pupils with emotional and behavioural difficulties adaptations 'are usually needed during the main teaching activity, with a shorter time for independent group work if adult support is not available' (ibid.). A pupil with severe or complex difficulties 'may need to be supported with an individualised programme in the main part of the lesson' (ibid.).

For pupils working below level 1 of the National Curriculum, published guidance offers examples of what pupils with SEN should be able to do at each performance description level (P level) (DfES, 2001d).

The national strategy for Key Stage 3: literacy, numeracy and SEN

Literacy in Key Stage 3

The national strategy for Key Stage 3 includes approaches to improve standards in literacy and numeracy across the curriculum (DfEE, 2001a: 2001b). *Literacy Across the Curriculum* (DfEE, 2001a) provides materials for in-service education and training (INSET) aiming to raise literacy standards. The literacy strand of the Key Stage 3 National Strategy is organised around the 'Framework for Teaching English: Years 6, 7 and 8'. The framework, organised in terms of word, sentence and text-level objectives, gives attention to reading, writing and speaking and listening and highlights key objectives essential to literacy development (ibid.: 4). All subject teachers are expected to plan, teach and mark according to the key objectives. Cross-curricular priorities are identified for Years 7–9.

While there is some reference to inclusive classrooms, the focus is on pupils for whom English is an additional language. Where there is a particular concentration on SEN, it concerns special schools.

Numeracy in Key Stage 3

A *Numeracy Across the Curriculum* pack was also intended to support INSET. It was suggested that, where schools have a Key Stage 3 management group, it should oversee development in numeracy. As part of the approach, schools devoted a training day in spring 2002 to learning how to improve pupils' numeracy skills and encouraging pupils to develop and use them appropriately in other subjects. Schools were advised to identify cross-curricular activities for each of Years 7–9 under priority headings (for example, to improve accuracy, particularly in calculation, measurement and graphical work) (DfEE, 2001b).

Among questions the secondary school was encouraged to consider were the following:

- 'What simplifications/modifications are made for pupils with specific learning difficulties?'
- 'Are teaching assistants aware of supporting resources, such as number lines, hundred squares, place-value charts, vocabulary checklists?'

■ 'Have you considered pre-tutoring pupils who are experiencing difficulties so that they can participate in the lesson with their peers and with a little more confidence?' (ibid.: Handout 3.12, Unit 3, p. 101).

Learning support assistants

While Balshaw (1999) raises the issue of pupils becoming overdependent on the learning support assistant (LSA), the importance and complexity of the LSA's work are widely recognised. LSAs fulfil different functions by working in a differentiated way within the classroom, either with individuals or with groups. Also, where the LSAs are working with individual pupils rather than working with small groups or where they are modifying materials outside the classroom, they fulfil further roles. Heeks and Kinnell (1997: 49–50) distinguish eight roles: interpreter, scribe, organiser, motivator, partner, accessor, reinforcer, and emotional and behavioural helper. An important function of the LSA in relation to individually orientated approaches to teaching and learning is to reinterpret or restructure what the teacher has presented – a complex and subtle task.

Particularly in relation to the literacy hour, it has been suggested that teachers regard the presence of another adult in the classroom as essential if the literacy hour is to be successful (Gordon, 1999: 57–9). Group time lends itself most readily to the support of an LSA as the focus can be on the particular requirements of a specified group (Lingard, 2000). In whole-class sections of the literacy hour (or the numeracy session), the LSA can provide support that is less direct, such as encouraging contributions from a reluctant pupil or helping sustain the concentration of a particular pupil through encouraging him or her discretely.

Learning support can have the effect of enhancing the quality of teaching and learning in the classroom and can provide extra flexibility to draw on and adapt the teaching and learning approaches outlined earlier. However, if the structure of the numeracy session and the literacy hour is regarded as a strength, flexibility has to be within parameters that do not sacrifice the advantages of that structure.

Thinking points

Practitioners may wish to consider:

■ the role of psychology in underpinning approaches to teaching and learning;
■ the relationship between broad curriculum requirements and individualistic approaches to teaching and learning and the extent to which these can be reconciled; and

- the importance of whole class and group work as well as individual approaches.

Key text

Leadbetter, J., Morris, S., Timmins, P., Knight, G. and Traxon, D. (1999) *Applying Psychology in the Classroom*. London: David Fulton.

10

National Frameworks: Further Clarity

Introduction

Two aspects of the national framework for SEN may be distinguished: the organisations involved, and the legislation, guidance and perspectives within which special education operates. This chapter outlines the organisational roles of the DfES SEN Division, OfSTED, the Teacher Training Agency (TTA) and the Qualifications and Curriculum Authority (QCA). It then considers recent guidance and related legislation, in particular the Special Educational Needs and Disability Rights in Education Act 2001, *The Special Educational Needs Code of Practice* (DfES, 2001a) and *Inclusive Schooling: Children with Special Educational Needs* (DfES, 2001e).

Inter-relationships between national, local and school frameworks

Chapters 10–12 consider, respectively, national, local and school frameworks. These are inter-related and are divided for ease of explanation. National legislation, such as the Special Educational Needs and Disability Rights in Education Act 2001, has local and school implications. *The Special Educational Needs Code of Practice* (DfES, 2001a) affects LEAs, schools and others. Local frameworks that aim to develop closer liaison between services and others often relate to national initiatives – Schools Plus, Excellence in Cities and Sure Start being examples.

School frameworks are influenced by national and local developments. Schools' SEN policies follow guidance and regulations provided nationally. The roles of governors, SENCOs, teachers and teaching assistants and their relationships with parents are informed by the nationally developed *Special Educational Needs Code of Practice* (DfES, 2001a) and other guidance. School curriculum and assessment are guided by national requirements. Developments in individual schools and across LEAs are disseminated to provide examples of good practice. The inter-relatedness of the national, local and school frameworks enables innovation to take place, within certain parameters.

Organisations

The DfES SEN Division

The aim of the DfES was expressed when it was still known as the Department for Education and Employment. It is to 'give everyone the chance, through education, training and work, to realise their full potential, and thus to build an inclusive and fair society and a competitive economy' (DfEE, 2001c: 2). The role of the DfES SEN Division, as indicated in the division's mission statement in its business plan, concerns standards, participation, leadership, inclusive practice, integrated provision, access and equality of opportunity and supporting services. Specifically, it involves the following:

- Campaigning for high standards and high expectations for all children with SEN.
- Being advocates for full participation by all young people in post-16 education, training and employment.
- Providing teachers, schools, early years settings and LEAs with leadership and advice to ensure that children with SEN have those needs met.
- Promoting inclusive practice which enables all children to play a full part in the life of the school, mix with their peers and prepare for adult life.
- Joining with all interested agencies and services (voluntary, private and state) to create integrated provision for children with SEN.
- Securing access and equality of opportunity for disabled children in schools and in early years settings.
- Supporting services for the parents of children with SEN.

Teacher Training Agency

A principal aim of the Teacher Training Agency (TTA) – to promote effective and efficient professional development for teachers and headteachers – is focused upon improvements in the quality of teaching and leadership that are expected to have the maximum impact on pupils' learning. A major feature of this work is the development of national standards for the teaching profession to define expertise in key roles. Some of these are considered below.

The standards for the award of Qualified Teacher Status, the *QTS Standards* (TTA, 2002a), include many requirements that have a bearing on SEN as well as ones that relate directly to SEN. For example, one standard requires that teachers must demonstrate that: 'They understand their responsibilities under the *SEN Code of Practice*, and know how to seek advice from specialists on less common types of special educational needs' (ibid.: Standard 2.6). The statutory *Induction Standards* (TTA, 2002b) include a requirement that newly qualified teachers, by the end of the induction period: 'plan effectively, where applicable, to meet the needs of pupils with SEN, with or without statements, and in consultation with the SENCO contribute to the preparation, implementation, monitoring and review of Individual Education Plans or the equivalent' (ibid.: standard (g)). *Understanding Special Educational Needs: A Guide for Student Teachers* (Farrell, 2003) explores and develops the SEN implications of the *QTS Standards* and *Induction Standards*.

The *National Standards for Special Educational Needs Co-ordinators* (TTA, 1998a) concern the core purpose of the SENCO, key outcomes of SEN co-ordination, professional knowledge and understanding, skills and attributes, and key areas of SEN co-ordination. They are supplemented by guidance setting out examples of ways of using the SENCO standards: These cover using the standards:

■ for performance review;
■ to deploy staff effectively;
■ in recruitment;
■ to inform policy and practice at school level and to evaluate its effectiveness;
■ to inform training; and
■ for strategic planning at the regional level (TTA, 2000).

The *standards* aim to help the school identify training and development needs relating to the effective teaching of pupils with severe and/or complex SEN. They concern headteachers and teachers in mainstream schools; teachers and managers of special classes and of units in mainstream schools; staff in special schools and pupil referral units; and teachers and managers in support services (TTA, 1999).

Qualifications and Curriculum Authority

The Qualifications and Curriculum Authority (QCA), in its remit for developing and refining the National Curriculum, recognises two aims of the National Curriculum. These are that all maintained schools provide a balanced and broadly based curriculum that:

■ promotes the spiritual, moral, cultural, mental and physical development of pupils at the school and of society; and
■ prepares pupils at the school for the opportunities and responsibilities of adult life.

A framework sets out curriculum guidance for the Foundation stage of education (QCA/DfEE, 2000). Advice on providing for pupils with SEN includes that the teacher's focus should be on 'removing barriers for children where these already exist and on preventing learning difficulties developing' (ibid.: 18). Practitioners should take specific action to help children with SEN make the best possible progress by providing for those requiring help with communication, language and literacy skills, and planning as necessary to develop understanding through all available senses and experiences. Teachers should plan for full participation in learning and in all practical and physical activities. They should help children with behavioural difficulties take part in learning, by, for example, 'encouraging and promoting positive behaviour' (ibid.: 19).

The QCA's inclusion statement identifies three principles for inclusion: setting suitable learning challenges; responding to pupils' diverse learning needs; and overcoming potential barriers to learning and assessment for individuals and groups of pupils (QCA/DfEE, 1999a: 30–6). Other guidance includes that relating to target setting for pupils with learning difficulties (e.g. QCA/DfEE, 2001a; 2001b).

Office for Standards in Education (OfSTED)

OfSTED's aim is 'to help improve the quality and standards of education through independent inspection and advice' (2001: Introduction, para. 1). The Schools Inspections Act 1996 and other legislation makes provision for the regular inspection of all state-funded schools in England. Her Majesty's Chief Inspector of Schools has a duty to secure that every appropriate school in England is inspected at prescribed intervals by a 'registered' inspector. The SEN responsibility for school inspections includes inspecting SEN provision in mainstream schools as well as special schools and pupil referral units. The focus is indicated in such documents as its framework for inspection (OfSTED, 2003a) and in handbooks used by both schools and inspectors (OfSTED, 2003b; 2003c; 2003d).

Earlier guidance from the then Department for Education and Employment considered social inclusion in terms of pupils who were likely to be excluded from school. *Circular 10/99* concerned the support of pupils at risk of exclusion and who may become disaffected (DfEE, 1999b), while *Circular 11/99* concerned the role of LEA support for these children (DfEE, 1999c). However, OfSTED guidance (2000) to inspectors and schools indicates a wider definition of inclusion. The OfSTED document considers educational inclusion as more than 'a concern about any one group of pupils such as those who have been or are likely to be excluded from school' (ibid.: 1). The groups to which this definition of inclusion applies include:

- girls and boys;
- minority ethnic and faith groups, travellers, asylum seekers and refugees; and
- pupils who need support to learn English as an additional language.

In summary, inclusion refers to all pupils.

But a potential difficulty in making the inclusion net so wide is that the particular requirements of pupils with SEN (and other particular groups) may be insufficiently addressed. It could be argued that children and young people are not defined by their SEN in isolation but by other features such as their ethnic group and whether their family is under stress, and that to recognise this is to provide better for the whole child. Even so, is also important that the particular knowledge and skills associated with providing for pupils with SEN are not overlooked in an approach that is so broad as to 'include' everyone.

▊ Recent government approaches

Background

Of central importance in current SEN legislation is the legal definition of SEN in the Education Act 1996 and related terminology, such as 'learning difficulty', 'difficulty in learning' and 'disability', which were discussed in Chapter 2. The contextual nature of the definition of SEN and the consequent importance of developing locally agreed criteria were indicated there.

Recent government approaches to SEN in England have been indicated in a range of documents. Following an earlier white paper *Excellence in Schools* (DfEE, 1997b) that had to do with education generally, the green paper *Excellence for All Children: Meeting Special Educational Needs* (DfEE, 1997a) concerned raising standards, shifting resources to practical support and increasing inclusion. It was succeeded by the document *Meeting Special Educational Needs: A Programme of Action* (DfEE, 1998b) which set out a time schedule proposing action for three years (1998–2001), including revising the *Special Educational Needs Code of Practice* – (DfES, 2001a).

Special Educational Needs and Disability Rights in Education Act 2001

The Special Education Needs and Disability Rights in Education Act 2001 (SENDA) provides an example of legislation that includes checks and balances regarding grounds for discrimination. SENDA amends the Disability Discrimination Act 1995 and the Education Act 1996 and it makes further provision against discrimination on grounds of disability in schools and other educational establishments. SENDA provisions for SEN apply to England and Wales. Provisions relating to the rights of disabled people in education concern England, Wales and Scotland (except the duty to produce an accessibility strategy or plan, which does not apply to Scotland). SENDA is supplemented by a *Code of Practice* concerning Part IV of the Disability Discrimination Act 1995 in schools (Disability Rights Commission, 2001a) and a *Code of Practice* for the post-16 sector (Disability Rights Commission, 2001b).

Part 1 of SENDA amends the Education Act 1996 for children with SEN. It strengthens the right of children with SEN to be educated in mainstream schools but a balance is indicated between this and other factors. The 'right' should not be incompatible with the wishes of the child's parents or the provision of efficient education for other children. However, the LEA must show that there are no reasonable steps they could take to prevent the incompatibility.

Part 2 of SENDA places duties on LEAs and schools, including independent and non-maintained special schools, in England and Wales. It sets duties on local authorities, independent schools, self-governing schools and grant-aided schools in Scotland. It is unlawful for a responsible body of a school to discriminate against a disabled child who might become a pupil at the school in relation to its admission arrangements, exclusions or in the education or associated services provided for or offered to pupils at the school. Three aspects taken together constitute unlawful discrimination. These are that the less favourable treatment is for a reason that is directly related to the child's disability; is less favourable treatment than someone gets if the reason does not apply to him or her; and cannot be justified. Less favourable treatment may be justified if it is the result of a permitted form of selection or is for both a material and substantial reason.

A second key duty is to make reasonable adjustments to admission arrangements, exclusions and in relation to education and related services to ensure that disabled pupils (or prospective pupils) are not substantially disadvantaged in comparison with their non-disabled peers, without justification. 'Reasonable adjustments' do not require the responsible body to provide auxiliary aids and services. For schools in the public sector, these will be made through the SEN framework. Nor do 'reasonable adjustments' require the responsible body to make physical alterations to the buildings. These are covered by the new planning duties. Generally a school cannot wait until a disabled pupil arrives before making an adjustment. The only justification for not making a reasonable adjustment is that there is a material and substantial reason.

The Act also provides for the possibility that a parent or child may request that the school keep confidential the fact that the child has a disability. In considering what reasonable adjustments to make, a responsible body must keep in mind the extent to which taking a particular step is consistent with maintaining confidentiality, where this has been requested. The Special Educational Needs and Disability Tribunal is the body to which appeals are made if it is considered that there has been unlawful discrimination.

A hierarchy of provision and individual pupils' SEN

The *Special Educational Needs Code of Practice* (hereafter the code) (DfES, 2001a) provides practical guidance to various parties about their responsibilities towards children with SEN. These parties include LEAs and the governing bodies of all schools for which the LEA has financial and administrative responsibility (that is, maintained schools).

The 'principles and policies' explain that the code provides practical guidance on the discharge of functions under the Education Act 1996. Those affected include LEAs, the governing bodies of all maintained schools, providers of government-funded early education and those who help them, including health and social services.

The code sets out guidance on policies and procedures seeking to enable pupils with SEN to reach their full potential; to be fully included in their school communities; and to make a successful transition to adulthood. A fundamental principle is that children with SEN 'should have their needs met' (code 1.5). A critical success factor is that the 'culture, practice, management and development of resources in a school or setting should be designed to ensure that all children's needs are met' (ibid.: 1.6) Other themes in the code include partnership with parents, pupil participation and interagency working.

The code indicates a graduated (in practice, hierarchical) approach to providing resources/support in the early years in the primary and the secondary phases, and in relation to statutory assessment and statement of SEN. Regarding early education settings, the government's Early Learning Goals set out what most children will achieve in various areas such as communication, language and literacy by the time they enter Year 1 of primary education. The identification of SEN is related to slow progress in the Foundation stage of education (for children from 3 to 5 years old). The provider intervenes through Early Years Action and, if progress remains unsatisfactory, the SENCO may seek advice and support from external agencies through Early Years Action Plus. Triggers are proposed for intervention through Early Years Action – for example, a child 'continues working at levels significantly below those expected for children of a similar age'. For communication and/or interaction difficulties, the child may require 'specific individual interventions' to access learning. Triggers are also indicated for outside intervention through Early Years Action Plus.

Concerning identification, assessment and provision in the primary and the secondary phases of education, the code sets out triggers for School Action and School Action Plus. Triggers for School Action all assume that the pupil has received differentiated learning opportunities. School Action Plus triggers assume that pupils are already receiving an individual programme and/or concentrated support.

The Code provides guidance to LEAs on the statutory assessment of SEN, which has to do with the duties of a LEA under the Education Act 1996. The LEA must identify and make a statutory assessment of those children for whom they are responsible who have SEN and who probably need a statement. If a school requests a statutory assessment on a child, it must provide supporting evidence. The code also gives guidance relating to statements of SEN and annual reviews.

Broad areas of SEN are identified. The code points out that these are not rigid and that there may be considerable overlap between them. The areas are communication and interaction; cognition and learning; behaviour, emotional and social development; and sensory or physical impairment. A further guidance document originally appended to the draft SEN code emerged from research by the Special Needs Research Centre at the University of Newcastle upon Tyne: *SEN Thresholds* (DfEE, 2000h). The document indicates thresholds for School Action and School Action Plus in the four areas mentioned.

In the threshold document, communication and interaction difficulties are regarded in relation to speech and language difficulties and to autistic spectrum disorders. Cognition and learning are considered in terms of general and specific learning difficulties. Lower and higher levels of general learning difficulty are indicated according to performance and attainment. Behavioural, emotional and social difficulties are considered at lower and higher levels of difficulty while, in a general description, age-inappropriate behaviour is given as an indication. Sensory and physical difficulties are considered as hearing impairment, visual impairment, and physical and medical difficulties.

While the code concerns a hierarchy of provision, it also relates to a continuum of SEN: the so-called graduated approach. This is defined in the glossary to the code (p. 203) as:

> A model of action and intervention in schools and early education settings to help children who have special educational needs. The approach recognises that there is a continuum of special educational needs and that, where necessary, increasing specialist expertise should be brought to bear on the difficulties that a child may be experiencing.

The SEN is identified and the response to it is eventually to try more intensive provision (Early Years Action or School Action). If this does not improve progress sufficiently or enable access to learning and the curriculum, more intensive provision is tried (Early Years Action Plus or School Action Plus). It may be necessary, in a small minority of cases requiring even higher levels of intervention, to issue a statement of SEN.

Such provision is deemed necessary because a pupil has difficulties in learning that lead, in the legal sense, to learning difficulties and the pupil is not making sufficient progress. Alternatively, the pupil has a disability that leads to a learning difficulty that requires special educational provision to be made. In other words, although the code may sometimes express itself in terms of level of provision, it cannot escape the fact that this is, and has, to be related to the level of learning difficulty or degree of disability in order that it is not capricious or random. LEAs need to determine what these levels will be in terms of criteria in agreement with parents, schools and others.

LEAs, schools, parents and others need to give careful consideration to the hierarchy of provision indicated by Early Years/School Action, Early Years/School Action Plus and statements of SEN. Provision, even if it is hierarchical, is only determined once there is agreement on the levels of learning difficulty and the local provision for disability that necessitate it.

Inclusion and parental preference for mainstream or special schools

A limited conception of inclusion emerged from the green paper on special education, *Excellence for All Children* (DfEE, 1997a). The implicit view was that inclusion is to do with including pupils by placing them in mainstream rather than special schools. 'Exclusion' appeared to be associated with attendance at a special school. The green paper regarded the peers of pupils with SEN as children in mainstream schools, referring to 'strong educational as well as social and moral grounds for educating children with SEN with their peers' (ibid.: 43).

A more recent document that sets out statutory guidance concerning inclusion is *Inclusive Schooling: Children with Special Educational Needs* (DfES, 2001e). The document points out the intention of the Special Educational Needs and Disability Act 2001 (in amending s. 316 of the Education Act 1996 and in inserting a new s. 316A) to give a strengthened 'right' to a mainstream education for children with SEN (ibid.: para. 4).

Inclusive schools and LEAs have: 'an inclusive ethos; a broad and balanced curriculum for all pupils; systems for early identification of barriers to learning and participation; and high expectations and suitable targets for all children' (ibid.: para. 8). The guidance (DfEE, 2001d: para. 11) explains the new duties of schools and LEAs under SENDA to prevent discrimination:

a. not to treat disabled pupils unfavourably, without justification, for a reason which relates to their disability;

b. make reasonable steps to ensure that disabled pupils are not placed at a substantial disadvantage compared to other pupils who are not disabled (but there is no duty to remove or alter physical features or provide auxiliary aids or services); and

c. also plan strategically for and make progress in improving the physical environment of schools for disabled children, increasing disabled pupils' participation in the curriculum and improving ways in which written information which is provided to pupils who are not disabled is also provided to disabled pupils.

The statutory framework for inclusion does not apply to certain children, including those:

- taught at home;
- receiving in-patient psychiatric treatment;
- in secure accommodation (ibid.: para. 8).

It may not be possible to take steps to prevent a child's inclusion being incompatible with the efficient education of others. For example:

- when a child's behaviour systematically, persistently and significantly threatens the safety of others;
- when a child's behaviour systematically, persistently and significantly impedes the learning of others; or
- where the teacher, even with other support, had to spend a greatly disproportionate amount of time with the child in relation to the rest of the class.

Where a child has a statement of SEN there is a general duty to educate the child in a mainstream school unless this would be incompatible with parental wishes or the provision of efficient education for other children. If placing a child in mainstream is considered incompatible with providing efficient education for other children, the LEA and the school need to provide evidence why no reasonable steps can be taken to prevent that incompatibility.

Parents may express a preference for a particular mainstream school to be named on their child's statement. If so, the LEA must name the school unless:

- the school cannot provide for the child's needs;
- including the child would be incompatible with the efficient education of other pupils; or
- including the child would be incompatible with the efficient use of resources.

Should the LEA not name the parents' preferred school, it must name another mainstream school.

Parents may ask for an independent mainstream school (e.g. a city technology college) to be named in their child's statement. The LEA must educate the child according to the parents' wishes so long as this is compatible with:

■ providing efficient education and training;
■ avoiding unreasonable public expenditure; and
■ meeting the normal admission criteria set by the school.

If the LEA does not name the independent mainstream school, it must name another mainstream school.

Should the parents not express a preference for a particular school, the LEA must decide which mainstream school is named in the child's statement. In any of the three scenarios above, parents have a right of appeal to the SEN tribunal. Parents may express a preference for special school to be named in their child's statement. If it is a particular maintained special school, the LEA must name the preferred school in the statement unless:

■ the school cannot provide for the child's needs;
■ including the child would be incompatible with the efficient education of other pupils; or
■ including the child would be incompatible with the efficient use of resources.

Should the LEA not name the parents' preferred school, it may name another school in the statement. The LEA must educate the child according to the parents' wishes so far as this is compatible with:

■ providing efficient education and training; and
■ avoiding unreasonable public expenditure.

Parents may request a non-maintained or independent special school to be named in their child's statement. The LEA must educate the child according to parental wishes in so far as this is compatible with the two criteria set out above. Where the LEA does not agree to name the non-maintained special school, it must name another school. If the parents do not express a preference for an individual special school to be named, the LEA must educate the child according to parental wishes in so far as this is compatible with the same two criteria set out above. In all the above cases, the LEA must also have regard to the need to arrange suitable educational provision imposed by s. 324 of the Education Act 1996.

Inclusive Schooling: Children with Special Educational Needs (DfES, 2001e) is intended to provide statutory guidance on the practical operation of the statutory framework for inclusion. However, it is difficult not to perceive a lack of even-handedness regarding parental wishes for a mainstream or special school place. This is perhaps best indicated where it is stated that: 'where parents want a mainstream education for their child everything possible should be done to provide it' (ibid.: para. 4). The document goes on to say that 'equally where parents want a special school place their wishes should be listened to and taken into account' (ibid.). The gap between doing 'everything possible' to provide a mainstream place and listening and taking into account the wishes of parents who want a special school place is made more apparent by their being connected by the word 'equally', as if they meant the same thing.

Yet in 2001 in a debate on the Special Educational Needs and Disability Bill, the then Schools Minister stated that special schools had nothing to fear. She said:

> although the size of the special school sector dropped from serving 1.3% of children in 1991 to 1.2% in 1995, it has remained constant in each of the last six years, catering for 1.2% of all our children or roughly 97,000 pupils. We do not envisage that it will change dramatically.

It appears that the position is an odd one: SEN inclusion will encourage mainstream placements but special school places will remain about the same. This could be the case if increasing numbers of children already in mainstream schools are identified as having SEN that requires a statement. This might be one reason why the proportion of pupils with SEN in mainstream schools is increasing while the number of pupils in special schools is expected to remain fairly static.

Suggestions for further developments

Among the strengths of the national framework in England is that it is underpinned by:

- policy responsibility through the SEN Policy Division of the DfES;
- a National Curriculum and assessment structure;
- standards for teachers and others that, in varying degrees, reflect requirements for SEN; and
- a regular cycle of inspection through OfSTED.

Among areas for further development are issues relating to the *Special Educational Needs Code of Practice* (DfES; 2001a) concerning links between provision and SEN and clarity concerning parental preferences for mainstream or special schools.

Thinking points

Practitioners working in an LEA setting may wish to consider whether their LEA:

- is clear about the triggers relating to SEN and about the implications of a hierarchy of provision to a greater level of learning difficulty or disability requiring provision over and above what is generally given;
- has a clear view of the role of its special and mainstream schools; and
- respects equally the views of parents wishing a mainstream place and parents wishing a special school place.

▓ Key texts

The Special Educational Needs and Disability Rights in Education Act 2001.
Department for Education and Skills (DfES) (2001) *Special Educational Needs Code of Practice.* London: DfES.
Department for Education and Skills (2001) *Inclusive Schooling: Children with Special Educational Needs.* London: DfES.

Local Frameworks: Closer Liason

Introduction

This chapter considers the role of the modern LEA within the context of partnership working and school improvement. It looks specifically at school
effectiveness and improvement in relation to SEN. The chapter examines
examples of liaison and joint working, including links across and within
services, SEN regional partnerships, the learning and Skills Council, Schools
Plus, Excellence in Cities, Sure Start and joint working in relation to speech
and language provision.

The role of the modern LEA

Key terms for the modern LEA are co-operation, partnership, regional collaboration, co-ordinated provision, flexibility and multi-agency working in the
context of supporting schools to raise standards and promote social inclusion. This is not new for, as Lacey (2000: 157) points out, there have been
decades of 'exhortations and initiatives' regarding multi-agency and multidisciplinary work for children with SEN.

   The importance of effective liaison between local services (such as the LEA,
social services and health services), and learning support councils and
between these and voluntary bodies and the private sector is currently being
being stressed. Regarding public bodies, *Meeting Special Educational Needs: A
Programme of Action* (DfEE, 1998b: annex A, 43) stated: 'There will be
improved co-operation between local education authorities, social services
departments and health authorities, with the focus on meeting children's
needs more effectively.' Strategically, the LEA is expected to maintain the
capacity to develop policy, set priorities, allocate resources and draw up plans
for delivery in relation to the authority's central functions. It is encouraged
to test out new ways of discharging its responsibilities in partnership with
other LEAs and with bodies in the public, private and voluntary sectors.

The LEA is expected to give a full account to schools (and to local council taxpayers) of the money they receive, including money delivered through spending assessment and through specific grants. LEA accounts indicate the proportion of funding that comes from central government and the proportion that comes through locally raised finance. The LEA has to take decisions 'in consultation with schools, about the distribution of the schools budget to take account of schools' differing needs.' (DfEE, 2000d: 7, para. 11). The LEA should identify and disseminate good practice and work within a more open market for school services. This may include offering schools an independent 'brokerage' service, putting them in touch with various suppliers to achieve the best value from their delegated budgets (ibid.: 13, para. 24).

The LEA's remit in relation to schools is crystallised in the four 'fair funding' headings: special educational needs; access to school places; school improvement; and strategic management. One of the key roles of an LEA concerns statutory functions, particularly relating to SEN. Regional collaboration projects have been piloted to provide for pupils with a low incidence of SEN (SEN regional partnerships originally did this but their remit is now wider).

The LEA is responsible for 'ensuring that the individual needs of children are quickly and accurately identified and matched by appropriate provision' (ibid.: 7, para. 13a). It also operates an education psychology service and support teaching services, liasing and linking with social and health services and planning the use of resources 'so that individual children can benefit from co-ordinated provision through their school' (ibid.: 8, para. 13a).

The LEA gives schools that are succeeding more leeway for self-management than schools that are performing poorly. Conversely, schools causing concern are monitored and are the subject of intervention more than other schools. In relation to pupils with SEN, this indicates that the LEA monitors such indicators as standards of pupils' achievement and progress and intervenes as necessary.

Local public service agreements (agreements between a local authority and central government) aim to reward improvements in performance in key services provided by local authorities. One of the targets involves 'SEN inclusion' – that is, educating fewer pupils with SEN outside mainstream schools. Flexibility is allowed by the DfES for local authorities who have set 'stretching' targets, including LEAs being able to transfer funding between Standard Fund categories. The development of these local public service agreements is part of the context for possible future models of local government (Clark, 2003).

Developments in the 'New Models' projects funded by the DfES indicate the direction of current thinking. For example, in Surrey LEA, the project (based on the scenario of a small strategic core LEA seeking to protect the 'rights' of children and of accountability) involves a new arrangement for LEA services, embracing competition and the principles of 'best sourcing'. Clusters of schools with greater delegated powers deliver services on a 'multi-agency basis' (see also Case Study 11.1).

Case Study 11.1 *Tower Hamlets New Models project*

The project in Tower Hamlets aimed to achieve a viable partnership model; improvements in such performance indicators as customer satisfaction and cost effectiveness; moves towards establishing best practice functions within customer/partner organisations; and the application more widely of knowledge management and networking processes.

Source: http://www.standards.dfes.gov.uk/lea/newmodels

The aim of having a slimmed-down, strategic LEA is indicated in the government white paper, *Schools Achieving Success* (DfES, 2001b). This seeks to secure a framework of support, challenge and a cost-effective service within which schools can concentrate on raising the standards of pupil achievement.

The role of the modern LEA is further indicated by the inspection regime for LEAs. The *Framework for the Inspection of Local Education Authorities* (OfSTED, 2002) provides the basis for LEA inspections by OfSTED and others, including staff of the Audit Commission. The regime includes the inspection of LEAs as an organisation, the inspection of themes (such as support for SEN provision) and the inspection of Best Value reviews of individual educational functions and services. The vital role of LEAs is seen as supporting schools in raising standards for all children and supporting social inclusion (guidance on inspection judgements is available at www.ofsted.gov.uk). Account is taken of the LEA's own self-evaluation of its work.

For the purposes of organisational inspection, the key functions of an LEA are grouped under the following headings:

- The LEA's strategy for school improvement.
- School improvement.
- SEN.
- Promoting social inclusion.
- Corporate issues (ibid. p.7).

Regarding SEN, the inspection considers the development and implementation of policies and strategies for SEN in order to meet statutory requirements, to analyse needs and audit current strengths and weaknesses, to identify LEA-wide targets for improvement and to set out plans and programmes to achieve these. The plans and programmes have to embody Best Value principles.

The inspection examines:

- the effectiveness of the LEA's strategy for SEN;
- the LEA's effectiveness in meeting its statutory obligations regarding SEN;

- the LEA's effectiveness in exercising its SEN functions to support school improvement; and
- the extent to which the LEA has exercised its SEN functions to secure value for money (ibid.: 10).

The inspection is followed by the publication of a report which includes recommendations that the LEA should consider in producing an action plan to improve its effectiveness. When LEAs are judged not to be performing satisfactorily, subsequent monitoring and intervention are greater than for other LEAs to help ensure that the inspection has the effect of improving services.

The Local Government Association and its partners, the National Health Service Confederation, Association of Directors of Social Services, Association of Chief Education Officers and Confederation of Education Directors, are working together on a new vision for children's services. This is set out in *Serving Children Well: A New Vision for Children's Services* (Local Government Association *et al.*, 2002). There are around 40 'pathfinder authorities' that have subscribed to this project. For example, Northumberland County Council is developing a mechanism to enable young people (including disabled young people), to help shape services relevant to them.

The vision of *Serving Children Well* is that providing a safe, supportive environment for children should be central to public services. It describes how local areas can co-ordinate and plan to meet children's needs, taking a multi-disciplinary approach to delivering services to minimise gaps in provision and to speed up responses. Key aspects are that:

- services for children are delivered within the accountable structure of the local government framework;
- there are shared outcomes and targets between agencies supported by joint inspections;
- there is joint commissioning across agencies and sectors;
- there is a single assessment process for children and families and efficient information sharing;
- there is a unified workforce plan for all those working with children; and
- children, families and communities are involved in planning and in setting priorities.

School effectiveness and improvement and SEN

School effectiveness research tries to identify whether various resources, processes and organisational arrangements affect outcomes for pupils. The research asks why some pupils in similar catchment areas progress better than others. The characteristics of schools as organisations are identified and form the rationale for interventions to improve schools. Such a model has been called the 'received model' (RM) (Lauder *et al.*, 1998). An effective school in these terms is 'one in which pupils progress further than might be expected from consideration of its intake' (Stoll and Mortimer, 1997: 10).

School effectiveness is more precisely defined if it specifies which outcomes are being considered (e.g. GCSE results, other forms of accreditation, personal and social development); what the timescale is; and to whom the outcomes apply (e.g. all pupils, most pupils, more able pupils) (Mortimore and Sammons, 1997). For Lunt and Norwich (1999: 78), in the RM effective schools are identified in terms of optimising outcomes for the majority of pupils. Because of this, there is 'the assumption that a minority, whatever its size, which we can assume to be those with special educational needs, will not be counted in identifying school effectiveness' (ibid: 14).

The concept of value added seeks to enable schools with pupils from lower socioeconomic levels to demonstrate their levels of performance (value added) in comparison with schools with pupils from higher socioeconomic backgrounds. Within this perspective, alternatives to the RM have been developed, including the 'contextual model' (CM) (Lauder *et al.*, 1998). The CM seeks to address what are considered to be some of the weaknesses of the RM. Some theorists have taken the view that improving schools will benefit pupils with SEN (Ramasut and Reynolds, 1993), while others are more cautious.

A key question is: 'Are schools which maximise outcomes for a minority with difficulties and disabilities also those that maximise for the majority?' In considering this question, an early study by Lunt and Norwich (1999) analysed the then Department for Education and Employment data on GCSE results from 1998 league tables and indicators of SEN in 3,151 secondary maintained mainstream schools. The question considered was 'do schools with more pupils with SEN have lower attainment levels in the league tables?' (ibid.: 53). The study indicated that 'the higher the performance of the school the lower the proportion of pupils with SEN' (ibid.: 65), although the authors counsel caution in the interpretation of the data given that the figures were for one year only.

Lunt and Norwich emphasise the importance of recognising different and perhaps conflicting values in debates about including pupils with SEN. They indicate that inclusion 'is not the only value in education and does not necessarily always promote opportunities for learning' (ibid.: 80). A single focus on inclusion 'can emphasise place over instructional substance and confuse participation with real opportunity' (ibid.).

Examples of liaison and joint working

Links across and within services

Worthington (2000: 34) indicates the more common links across and within services. In the education services, education psychologists have particular links with the children's service part of the local social services and with the health community services. Education welfare officers work especially closely with social service childcare officers. The education learning support service, the hospital paediatrician and the social services disability service work together. Teachers for pupils with hearing or visual impairment liase with specialist doctors in hospitals.

Teachers of pupils with language impairments forge links with speech and language therapists, and teachers of children with physical impairments work with occupational therapists. Those offering a portage service for pre-school children work with health visitors and staff in social services day nurseries. Education behaviour support services work closely with staff in child and adolescent mental health. In the education service, the education officers dealing with statements of SEN, the parent partnership officers, the voluntary named person group, the staff of pupil referral units, the home tuition service staff and hospital teachers form their own links within and across services (ibid.).

Early years development and childcare partnerships use interagency planning to bring together early years education and social care. Health action zones and education action zones co-ordinate action on social disadvantage and additional support for pupils with SEN within a framework that often includes private sector help. But such initiatives do not offer solutions, only possible ways of working that need careful development and monitoring (see Case Study 11.2).

Case study 11.2 *St Helens' Advice and Resources Centre*

An example of multi-agency support is the St Helens' Advice and Resources Centre (DfEE, 1997a: 13–14), which supports children with SEN and their families from birth until the child begins school. A steering group comprises parents and representatives of the LEA, social services, the local National Health Service trust and voluntary organisations. Staff include teachers, medical staff, specialists in hearing impairment and visual impairment, therapists, an educational psychologist, a portage and outreach support service, a social worker and a nursery nurse. Activities include an assessment nursery, a parent and toddler group, a communication group, a behaviour education and management group and a group for children with Down's syndrome and their parents.

SEN regional partnerships

The SEN regional partnerships established by the then Department for Education and Employment have encouraged the discussions of issues concerning provision for particular groups of children (DfES/DoH, 2002(a): 74–5). The partnerships bring together LEAs, local health and social services and the voluntary and private sectors (see Case Study 11.3).

Case study 11.3 *Examples of SEN Regional Partnerships*

- The West Midlands Partnership has concentrated on provision for children with autistic spectrum disorder and it produced a report looking at such issues as multi-agency working, terminology, diagnostic practice and the sharing of training placements (English and Essex, 2001).
- The Yorkshire and Humberside Partnership chose to work from a regional portfolio of effective SEN management to develop a regional consultancy register and a continuing professional development programme (DfES, 2002(d): 5).
- In the East Midland Partnership, an attempt has been made to enhance the education of children and young people in public care. A task group established a regional protocol drawing on research carried out by young people into the 'issues behind the statistics' (ibid.).

Learning and Skills Council

The Learning and Skills Council (LSC) is the body responsible for developing, planning, funding and managing post-16 education and training (except higher education) and work-based training for young people. In England, the LSC has local bodies that are responsible for raising standards and 'securing provision to match local learning and skills needs' (DfES, 2001(a): s. 10.18). With particular reference to SEN, the council, in meeting its responsibilities, must have regard to the needs of people with learning difficulties. It must take account of the assessments of people with learning difficulties arranged by the Connexions Service. A key objective of the council is planning to make sure that young people with learning difficulties or disabilities have access to high-quality learning.

Local learning and skills councils monitor local arrangements intended to meet the needs of young people with learning difficulties or disabilities. Joint working is important between the local learning and skills councils and the Connexions Service to make sure that suitable support and funding arrangements are in place for the provision that is set out in transition plans. This involves working with post-16 providers, schools and LEAs as necessary.

Building learning communities

One of 18 teams set up by the Social Exclusion Unit in 1998, the Schools Plus Policy Action Team identified and reported on approaches using schools as a focus for other community services and on reducing school failure. The report, *Schools Plus: Building Learning Communities* (Schools Plus Policy Action Team 11, 2000), indicated how staff in public services and others might work together more closely. The team considered education projects that most improve educational outcomes (such as homework centres and summer schools) and the best examples of mentoring and work experience schemes. They also supplied evidence that co-locating health and other social services at school level contributes to improved educational outcomes (ibid.: 8).

To raise pupil attainment, the team advocated extending school services that were offered to pupils. This included flexibility in the school system, such as that offered by study support or extended opening hours. In the development of summer schools through National Opportunity Funding (National Lottery money), it was expected that applications would give special attention to various groups, including children with SEN (ibid.: 26, para. 31). The report recognised that the programme would need to be linked to other funding streams, such as SEN funding (ibid.: recommendations, 28).

Other recommendations included extending the services offered on the school site through such means as one-stop family support centres. The report also recommended improving the quality and breadth of school–business links, perhaps through the wider use of mentors, through the use of 'local delivery agents' (to ensure that all schools have a framework for engaging pupils in work experience) and through contact with working adults. Another approach to raising attainment advocated by the team was greater school and community interaction. For example:

- Extending learning opportunities (for instance, through a neighbourhood learning centre offering resources and support for adult learners and study support opportunities for pupils);
- Recognising success in various ways, such as through a 'partnership with the community' award available to any primary, secondary or special school that meets the required standard.
- Extending and improving schools' links with parents (for example, by spreading existing family and learning support activities to more schools).
- Involving young people (for example, by developing and strengthening school councils).

Regarding links with parents, the report states that there is evidence that parental involvement in children's education has positive effects on attainment, claiming there is particular evidence of this in the field of SEN 'where relationships between school and parents are more formal' (ibid.: 45 para. 61). Concerning the involvement of young people in their communities, this is claimed to have advantages, including that it results in services being more responsive to the needs of individual groups, including those with SEN (ibid.: 47, para. 68).

Excellence in Cities

The Excellence in Cities programme (EiC) was introduced in 1999 to address the issue of low standards in many city schools (DfES, 2002e). Working in partnership was stressed. The only requirement for schools and local authorities to participate was that they should form a 'real partnership' (ibid.: 7) and develop delivery plans that would satisfy ministers. Networks (one of the expressions of the core EiC values) depend on 'schools working together collaboratively' (ibid.: 8). This includes sharing 'best practice' and tackling 'common problems' (ibid.: 9). The importance of collaboration is evident in its seven strands: opportunities for the gifted and talented, learning mentors, learning support units, city learning centres, beacon schools, EiC action zones and specialist schools.

Opportunities for gifted and talented pupils include the 'Excellence Challenge' for pupils over 16 that involves collaboration between schools and colleges. Learning mentors (who provide help for pupils facing 'barriers' to learning), form a single point of contact for accessing community and business programmes (such as out-of-school study support) and for accessing specialist support services, such as social and youth services, education welfare services, probation services and careers services. School-based learning support units working on behaviour and basic skills with disruptive pupils at risk of exclusion offer separate short-term teaching and support programmes. Many work closely with learning mentors and out-of-school support services (see Case Study 11.4).

Case study 11.4 *The Learning Support Unit, Benfield School, Newcastle*

The multi-agency work of the Learning Support Unit (LSU) at Benfield School, reported in *Excellence in Cities: Schools Extending Excellence Annual Report 2000–2001* (DfES, 2002e: 15), includes having one teaching room across the corridor from a second room where the education welfare officer joins the LSU manager and his assistant to provide for pupils who are more timid and frightened and tend to refuse school. Senior staff join the education welfare officer to visit targeted homes on particular evenings.

City learning centres (usually based on school sites) use information and communication technology to enhance learning – for example, by developing links with libraries and museums to provide expertise to students working on projects, and through video conferencing with schools in other counties to support the teaching of modern foreign languages. Beacon schools in EiC areas aim to contribute to raising standards through disseminating good practice and they offer a range of advice – some offering advice on SEN. In EiC action zones, schools and others collaborate to target additional resources on shared problems. Specialist schools place a particular focus on the teaching of technology, languages, sports and the arts.

Evaluations of EiC include an assessment of test and examination results. Improvements in Key Stage 3 tests in the year 2000–1 were a little stronger in EiC schools than in other non-EiC schools generally but, in English, they were four times stronger. Improvements in the percentage of pupils getting five or more A*–C grades in GCSE were a little greater in EiC schools than in other schools but, in London EiC schools, the improvement was better – some 3.8% improvement from 1999 to 2001 compared with 2.1% in non DfES, EiC schools (2002e: 33).

Sure Start

Another example of an approach that requires close partnership working is the Sure Start initiative (for a summary, see Forester and Stenson, 2001: 250–4), which provides universal services for children under 4 and their families living in disadvantaged communities. The programme seeks to improve the health and wellbeing of children and their families so that children can thrive when they reach school. Sure Start offers parents and would-be parents family support, advice on nurturing, health services and early learning. This may include outreach visiting, support for families and parents, support for play, learning and childcare for children; primary and community health care and support for children with SEN, including help in accessing specialist services.

The programmes are run by local partnerships. These draw together people from statutory agencies, voluntary and community organisations and parents to plan and organise local services. Sure Start offers the opportunity to inter-relate family policy and the early identification and support of pupils with SEN, particularly in disadvantaged communities. This requires the close collaboration of parents and professionals in the health, social and education services and others. The nature of the relationships in the Sure Start partnership is the most significant factor in setting up a local programme (Ball, 2002: 1) (see Case Study 11.5).

Case Study 11.5 *Examples of local activities supported by Sure Start*

■ Parents use a 'toolkit for babies' to help them develop their child's sound and speech development (Sheffield).
■ A free-phone helpline provides health and childcare advice to local parents every evening to 11 pm (Barrow).
■ Young homeless mothers living in a local hostel are offered play-and-stay sessions for their children while they receive health advice (Birmingham).

Source: Forester and Stenson (2001: 254).

In evaluations of Sure Start (Tunstill *et al.*, 2002), the programmes were considered to be making good use of multidisciplinary workers and existing health and social care professionals. It was recognised that 'joined-up working' is challenging and that, although some progress is being made, 'there is still a long way to go' (ibid.: 1). Specific evaluation is being made of one Sure Start objective ('improving children's ability to learn'), through the use of a Sure Start language measure. This is used to measure change in the language development of 2-year-olds in all Sure Start learning communities taken together and also in each individual Sure Start community (Harris, F. 2002: 1). In the first national baseline sample of November/December 2002, some 3% of the pupils had 'special needs' (ibid.: 2) (updated results are available at www.surestart.gov.uk).

Standards contract

The Local Government Association, the National Association of Independent Schools and Non-maintained Schools, the Association of Directors of Social Services and the DfES have completed a standards contract for the placement of pupils in day and residential independent and non-maintained schools. Both providers and purchasers can use this for new placements (www.nass-chools.org.uk). The National Association of Independent Schools and Non-maintained Schools is developing an agreed pre-placement protocol based on existing practice.

SEN Small Programmes Fund

The DfES SEN Small Programmes Fund promotes a 'one sector' approach to meeting pupils' SEN, supporting projects based on a commitment to working in partnership. It aims funding at projects that improve teaching and learning for pupils with SEN or disabilities, for sick children or for children who are looked after by the local authority. The fund aims to encourage a more strategic approach to working with the voluntary sector.

The three priorities for the fund are projects that:

1. have a positive and practical effect on practice in mainstream classrooms;
2. encourage a whole-school approach to inclusion and to meeting the needs of pupils with SEN; and
3. encourage a 'one sector' approach to providing for pupils with SEN or disabilities that helps redress the variations in the way such pupils are provided for.

The lead organisations that can apply for funding must be voluntary organisations or groups, or one of the SEN regional partnerships. Schools, LEAs, colleges, universities, health authorities, NHS trusts or social services are encouraged to be part of the consortium.

Speech and language therapy provision

Although much progress is being made, there are 'many reports of poor or non-existent joint work between agencies' (Lacey, 2000: 157). A particular example of the difficulties that are associated with liaison between services is the provision of speech and language therapy (SALT).

In 1998, the DfEE, DoH and the Welsh assembly set up a Speech and Language Therapy Working Group which reported two years later (DoH/DfEE, 2000). In 1999 the group also commissioned a study to 'map' existing provision across England and Wales to assist LEA and health service collaboration (Law *et al.*, 2001). While the remit of the working group was children receiving SALT, the study concerned all children with speech and language needs.

The research involved questionnaires, interviews and meetings. A survey of those responsible for SALT services indicated that caseloads and waiting lists for speech and language services were highest for children in the primary-school phase. About a fifth of SALT services have no SALT assistants, while over a half report difficulties in recruitment and retention. Some 60% of children receiving SALT services at the primary level have statements of SEN. A survey of those responsible for LEA services indicated that around 40% of children with statements of SEN have speech and language needs, while 10% of children with statements have speech and language needs as their primary need. Most LEAs (83–93%) had no specialist peripatetic provision.

Part of the difficulty with services for children with speech and language needs relates to the fact that speech and language services are located in health services (ibid.). While health services hold the prime responsibility for these, the 'ultimate' responsibility lies with the education service (R *v.* London Borough of Harrow). The lack of solution to this anomaly has been considered as an indictment of the failure of national level co-operative work (Dessent, 1996). The fact that LEA boundaries and health trust boundaries are coterminous in only 14% of cases further works against developing suitable frameworks for effective action.

Room for flexibility in the Health Act 1999 (ss. 29–31) provides for partnership arrangements between health bodies and local authorities. This is intended to encourage closer links between the health services provided by the National Health Service and the health-related functions of local authorities. The flexibility allows for pooled funding, lead commissioning and integrated provision (see Case Study 11.6).

Case Study 11.6 *Developing SALT in Bedfordshire and Portsmouth*

Bedfordshire organised a joint education and health service conference in 2002 on developing more effective services for children with speech and language needs. Subsequently, a working group was established to develop a better way of meeting the needs of these children. A further conference was held in 2003.

Portsmouth County Council uses the expertise of SALT in assessing children's needs and in advising on a suitable programme which is then delivered by language assistants. These assistants are trained through the school-based and LEA-funded annual training course. The training course was designed by (and is delivered by) SALT specialists and educational psychologists.

Following the report of the working group on the provision of SALT services to children with SEN (DfEE/DoH, 2000), a joint professional framework was developed (I-CAN, 2001). Intended to encourage closer liaison between teachers and speech and language therapists, the framework provides a structure to underpin joint training arrangements for the two professions. It does this, first, by defining areas of professional competence and knowledge, understanding and practical skills that enable the two professions to 'work effectively with the speech, language and communication needs ... of pupils in an educational setting' (ibid.: 5). Secondly, the framework provides an outline for continuing professional development that could be pursued 'jointly and collaboratively' by both teachers and speech and language therapists.

Thinking points

Practitioners may wish to consider:

- how their own LEA is placed to respond flexibly to modern demands and future developments;
- how effectively the LEA and the school is involved in liaison and joint working; and
- how effectively their local services are in responding to the challenge of co-ordinating speech and language services.

▌ Key texts

Local Government Association, National Health Service Confederation, Association of Directors of Social Services (2002) *Serving Children Well: A New Vision for Children's Services*. London: LGA, NHSC, ADSS.

Office for Standards in Education (2002) *Framework for the Inspection of Local Education Authorities*. London: OfSTED.

School Frameworks: Greater Flexibility

Introduction

This chapter discusses school SEN policy, looking at some of the key roles in schools concerning SEN: governors, staff in general SENCOs and teaching assistants. The roles and responsibilities of parents are also considered. The chapter goes on to consider the curriculum and school organisation in the context of including a wider range of pupils in mainstream schools. It then examines curriculum flexibility/differentiation, assessment and school organisation. Finally, it considers how individual education plans can be enhanced.

School SEN Policy

A school's SEN policy sets out the principles and practices of the school's approach to SEN. Policy implies a broad strategic view of provision that is a guiding influence. It involves having the correct documentation and, equally importantly, developing the policy through consultation to ensure that those following it understand and endorse it. The better the discussion and consultation in developing and refining the SEN policy, the greater the likelihood that staff will subscribe to it, understand it more fully and use it more productively. Parents and others will tend to support it. Ideally, policy should reflect practice, and practice should be an expression of policy.

SEN policy has to contain certain information specified in *Statutory Instrument 2506*: the *Education (Special Educational Needs) (Information) Regulations 1999* which form an appendix to the *Special Educational Needs Code of Practice* (DfES, 2001a). In early education settings and city academies, the SEN policy has to contain information as set out in the conditions of the grant. LEAs must ensure that pupil referral units have suitable SEN policies.

The governing body of a maintained mainstream school must publish information on the school's SEN policy and report on the policy and, at least annually, it must consider and report on its school policies and on the effectiveness of the school's work for pupils with SEN.

▌ Roles and duties

Governors

Governing bodies of all maintained schools (including those with nursery classes), have statutory duties regarding pupils with SEN. In liaison with the headteacher, the governing body determines the general policy of the school and its approach to meeting pupils' SEN (whether or not the pupils have a statement). Governing bodies establish appropriate staffing and funding arrangements and oversee the work of the school. The governing body may appoint a committee to monitor the school's work for pupils with SEN.

Under the School Standards and Framework Act 1998, governors are required to conduct the school so as to promote high standards. This concerns the standards of all pupils, including those with SEN. The *Special Educational Needs Code of Practice* (DfES, 2001a: ch. 1, s. 18) states that governors should ensure that objectives are set for the headteacher (using the performance management framework). The objectives (which should all apply to SEN and relate to school improvement plan priorities) include leadership and management and pupil achievement and progress.

Under the Education Act 1996, governing bodies have a legal duty to fulfil certain tasks. These are summarised in various booklets for governors published by the DfES. Governing bodies must make every effort to ensure that the necessary special arrangements are made for pupils with SEN. A 'responsible person' in each school has to ensure that everyone who is likely to teach a pupil with SEN is aware of these needs. While the 'responsible person' is normally the headteacher, it may be the chairperson of the governing body or another governor charged with that responsibility.

It is a duty of the governing body to make sure that teachers in the school are aware of the importance of identifying and providing for pupils with SEN. When it seems necessary or desirable in the interests of co-ordinated special educational provision in the area, the governing body must consult the LEA and other governing bodies. It must ensure that a pupil with SEN joins in school activities with pupils who do not have SEN, so far as is practical given certain provisos. The provisos are that this is compatible with the child receiving the special educational provision his or her learning needs require and the efficient education of pupils with whom they are taught. The governing body must report annually to parents on the implementation of the school's policy for pupils with SEN (DfEE, 2000e; 2000f) and must have regard to the *Special Educational Needs Code of Practice* (DfES, 2001a) when carrying out its duties towards all pupils with SEN.

As good practice, governors should establish procedures to make sure they are properly informed about the systems for within-school monitoring and evaluation and their outcomes. Governors should ensure they are fully involved in developing and monitoring the school's SEN policy. All governors, particularly any SEN governor, must be up to date and knowledgeable about the school's SEN provision, including how resources (personnel, money and equipment) are effectively and efficiently deployed. The governing body should make sure that SEN provision is a part of the school improvement plan and that the quality of SEN provision is properly monitored.

Governing bodies must make available to the LEA details of the arrangements the school makes for pupils with SEN. In preparing their education development plans, LEAs consult with the governing body and may ask for summary information on the incidence of pupils with SEN.

The National Association of Governors and Managers aims to improve the contribution of school governors to the quality of education provided by their school by providing advice, information and training. They produce publications relating specifically to SEN. The DfES Internet site has sections specifically for governors. Training in SEN issues may also be provided by an LEA officer or by an external consultant bought in by the LEA.

All staff

In early education settings in receipt of government funding (except for LEA-maintained schools, including nursery schools) provision for children with SEN concerns everyone in the setting. Key people are the headteacher or manager and the SENCO, but all staff bear responsibilities. The allocation of day-to-day responsibilities is determined by individual settings. The LEA retains the general duty to identify and make provision for children with SEN.

Concerning maintained mainstream primary and secondary schools, the governing body has functions which, in the case of maintained nursery schools, are carried out by the LEA. In all these maintained mainstream schools, provision for pupils with SEN concerns the whole school. Important functions are carried out by the governing body, the headteacher and the SENCO (or the SEN team). The school determines the allocation of day-to-day responsibilities, taking into account the circumstances of the school, its ethos, priorities and size.

Regarding special schools, the provision for pupils is a whole-school matter. The statutory duties remain with the governing body rather than the school staff, whatever the arrangements for meeting the needs of the pupils.

The SENCO

In early education settings, SENCOs ensure that liaison takes place with parents and professionals regarding children with SEN. They are responsible for advising and supporting other practitioners in the setting; seeing that appropriate individual education plans are in place; and making sure that background information on individual children with SEN is collected, recorded and kept up to date (*Special Educational Needs Code of Practice* – DfES, 2001a: 4.15).

In mainstream primary schools, the key responsibilities of the SENCO may include overseeing the day-to-day operation of the school's SEN policy and co-ordinating provision for pupils with SEN. Their responsibilities embrace liaising with other teachers and advising them; liasing with the parents of children with SEN; managing learning support assistants; overseeing the records of all children with SEN; contributing to the in-service training of staff; and liaising with external agencies (ibid.: 5.32). The responsibilities of SENCOs in secondary schools are similar (ibid.: 6.35).

The role of the SENCO in supporting developments in SEN is central (TTA, 1998a). Also important is the role of the headteacher (and other senior staff) in supporting the SENCO in his or her duties (TTA, 1998b). Without such support (unless the SENCO is a member of the senior management team) the whole-school aspects of the SENCO's duties are difficult to implement. The standards for SENCOs (TTA, 1998a) make clear the importance of the shared responsibility of the SENCO and the headteacher (and the governing body): 'The SENCO's fundamental task is to support the headteacher in ensuring that all staff recognise the importance of planning their lessons in ways that will encourage the participation and learning of all pupils' (ibid.: 5).

The teaching assistant

Teaching assistants assist the teacher in planning pupil's work, help to organise the classroom to facilitate differentiated work, assist in preparing curriculum materials, help with particular pupil tasks with individual pupils and provide support to keep children on task. They work with individuals or groups of children and contribute to and support the pupil's individual education plan (IEP). Teaching assistants provide additional explanations to children when necessary and support the teacher in general behaviour management. Reviewing individual pupil progress in collaboration with the teacher is another responsibility. Teaching assistants attend school briefings and professional development sessions and liase with parents where appropriate (Garner and Davies, 2001).

Given the variety and complexity of this role, it is perhaps not surprising if there are sometimes difficulties. A study of four schools suggested that in-class support is the commonest way of aiding inclusion. However, relationships between the teacher and teaching assistant were not always positive. Teachers sometimes resented the 'intrusion' of a teaching assistant, roles were often unclear and effective shared planning was rare (Clark *et al.*, 1999).

However, such potential difficulties make it all the more important that the teacher works closely with teaching assistants. While a teaching assistant may not work exclusively with pupils with SEN, he or she needs a good understanding of children with SEN. Joint planning is the ideal. Alternatively, the teacher should convey to the teaching assistant:

■ the overall 'picture' of the lesson and how it will develop, including its learning objectives;
■ the teaching and support strategies planned; and
■ the learning outcomes expected of the pupil whom the teaching assistant is supporting.

Assessments of what the pupil has done should be recorded so that this informs subsequent teaching.

Recent developments in the role of the teaching assistant include consultation on the role of support staff, including teaching assistants as indicated in the publication *Developing the Role of School Support Staff: The Consultation* (DfES, 2002f). In 2003, government, employers and workforce unions signed a national agreement in an attempt to free teachers to focus more on teaching and learning and raising standards. Changes are proposed for teachers and support staff responsibilities, including developing standards for higher-level teaching assistants.

Parents

The importance of the contribution of parents and that of effective liaison with the parents of children with SEN is recognised (Greenwood, 2002). Parents have responsibilities to help ensure that SEN provision is appropriate. If they are the parents of a child with SEN, they will take an interest in the individual provision and the progress of their own child, whether or not this involves the child receiving a statement. Where the child does have a statement, the parents will attend annual reviews where provision, progress and standards should be considered. The roles of parents (as set out in the *Special Educational Needs Code* – DfES, 2001a) are very much in this individual context. The 'Principles and practices' of the code include that 'special educational professionals take into account the **views of individual parents** in respect of **their child's particular needs**' (ibid.: code 1.6, emphasis in original).

The chapter 'Working with parents' touches on broader practice in referring to the need for LEAs to ensure that they are 'accessible, welcoming and value the views and involvement of parents' (ibid.: code 2.13). But much of the code reinforces concentration on individual pupils. Parents should:

■ recognise and fulfil their responsibilities as parents and play an active and valued role in their children's education;
■ have knowledge of their child's entitlement within the SEN framework;
■ make their views known about how their child is educated; and

■ have access to information, advice and support during assessment and any related decision-making process about special educational provision (ibid.: code 2.2).

In similar vein, professionals should 'acknowledge and draw on parental knowledge and expertise in relation to their child' (ibid.: Code 2.7). Parents should be 'fully involved in the school based response for their child' (ibid.: code 2.10). In working with schools, parents should 'communicate regularly with their child's school and alert them to any concerns they may have about their child's learning or provision' (ibid.: code 2.11).

While of course the main concern of any parent is with his or her own child, such concern is of limited value unless parents (or parent representatives) have an understanding of what the school should be achieving for pupils with SEN. Without a broad overview, it will not be possible to judge whether the individual progress and provision for any one child is or is not satisfactory. Such an overview may be obtained in two main ways. First, the parent governor can work closely with the SEN governor and others to ensure parents are provided with sufficient information to assess the school's provision for SEN. Secondly, at the annual meeting of parents and governors, parents should ensure that the SEN policy and provision are properly presented and discussed.

Among sources of support and information for parents is the Independent Panel for Special Education Advice (IPSEA), which offers free independent advice on appealing to the Special Educational Needs and Disability Tribunal and free, second, professional opinions.

The curriculum, school organisation and inclusion

Consideration has been given for some time to the ways in which the school curriculum and school and classroom organisation (and other factors) might be adapted to include more pupils in mainstream schools. The aim is to adapt schools to educate a wider range of pupils than at present, within the legal checks and balances relating to the inclusion of pupils in mainstream schools. For example, pupils may not be educated in mainstream schools if they seriously hinder the education of other pupils. Also, many parents of children with SEN continue to prefer that their children are educated in a special school or in a predominantly separate within-school unit rather than a mainstream school. From an international perspective (Evans, 2000: 70), it has been pointed out that few countries in the world have achieved 'the level of inclusion' whereby all pupils, no matter how seriously they are 'disadvantaged', can be supported effectively in mainstream classrooms.

Ainscow (1988) intimated that if too much attention is paid to analysing particular tasks for individual pupils this may constrain perspectives so that there is insufficient focus on other contextual features that may be hindering learning. These contextual features may be related to such factors as the curriculum or classroom organisation. Using findings from the UNESCO teacher education project, 'Special Needs in the Classroom', Ainscow (1995) went on to characterise the features that need to be present in a school if it intends to restructure to provide effective education for a wider range of pupils. These include that staff, pupils and members of the local community be involved in developing school policies and in making decisions. There should also be collaborative planning and co-ordination strategies.

In an American context, Lipsky and Gartner (1996) analysed the results of a study of inclusive educational programmes conducted by the National Center on Educational Restructuring and Inclusion. Among elements needed for inclusion to be effective were the development of collaborative planning teams and ensuring that time is made available for teachers to plan jointly. As well as adapting the curriculum, the pedagogy must be effective. Methods of assessment need to be developed and used in a way that enables pupils to show what they have learnt.

On the theme of collaborative working in the development of a holistic view of the curriculum, it was suggested by Lacey and Thomas (1993) that educators and health professionals should better share their expertise. Therapists based in schools might then develop a better grasp of curriculum requirements, while teachers might learn more about the therapeutic needs of particular children. This could lead to the development of a collaborative curriculum in which therapists and staff in the support services participate fully.

Such approaches have implications for how the curriculum is planned and presented and how the school is organised. For example, the development of school policy will involve greater consulatation about the curriculum than is customary. Strategies for co-ordination will have implications for teachers and others working together which, in turn, impacts on school and classroom organisation (including ensuring that time is made available to achieve these aims) (see Case Study 12.1).

Case Study 12.1 *Sele First School, Northumberland*

Sele First School is a beacon status community primary school that has worked on transition issues with primary and first schools, a middle school and high school. The school has sought to clarify the role of the SENCO and the monitoring of SEN provision to improve its quality. The school works with parents and all other schools in the local partnership to try to ensure that SEN is well managed and that there is good continuity. As a result of being involved in a shared placement scheme between special and mainstream schools, Sele First School has reviewed training provision for non-teaching staff, both within its LEA and beyond. This has resulted in the development of assessment portfolios and better systems of assessment and tracking of pupils with SEN.

Source: DfES (2002d: 4).

Curriculum flexibility/differentiation

Three principles for inclusion

The structure of the National Curriculum (NC) (QCA/DfEE, 1999a; 1999b) helps to ensure that, for all pupils, including those with SEN, there is a range and balance of different forms of curriculum experience. The curriculum structure has been publicly debated and modified in the light of experience, and the public nature of the document allows this process to continue. The flexibility of the NC was further enhanced by developments relating to a more inclusive curriculum. Three principles for inclusion are set out (QCA/DfEE, 1999a: 30–7; 1999b: 32–9).

1. Setting suitable learning challenges.
2. Responding to pupils' diverse learning needs.
3. Overcoming potential barriers to learning and assessment for individuals and groups of pupils.

Setting suitable learning challenges

In setting suitable learning challenges, teachers may choose knowledge, skills and understanding from earlier key stages so that pupils may make progress and demonstrate what they can achieve. This may mean there is not enough time to teach all aspects of age-related programmes of study. Greater differentiation of work will be needed for some pupils (QCA/DfEE, 1999a: 30–1; 1999b: 32–3). For example, for a pupil whose attainments are significantly below the expected levels at a particular key stage, differentiation may involve regarding the programmes of study as the wider context of learning while planning learning that is suitable for the pupil's requirements. The series of booklets on planning work for pupils with learning difficulties (e.g. QCA/DfEE, 2001b) is useful for this.

Responding to pupils' diverse learning needs

Responding to pupils' diverse learning needs, teachers plan for teaching and learning so that all pupils can participate in lessons. The teacher involves pupils by:

■ creating effective learning environments;
■ securing their motivation and concentration;
■ providing equality of opportunity through teaching approaches;
■ using appropriate assessment approaches; and
■ setting targets for learning (QCA/DfEE, 1999a: 31–3; 1999b: 33–5).

For example, teachers help to create effective learning environments by developing good relationships with pupils and building a classroom ethos in which the contributions of all pupils are valued and in which pupils feel secure enough to contribute. Any stereotyped views of pupils with SEN are challenged.

Motivation and concentration are secured by the teacher using approaches that take account of the different learning styles pupils may have. A pupil with specific learning difficulties can be taught using multisensory methods systematically involving vision, hearing, touch and movement. Resources can also be used that project positive images of children and adults with learning difficulties and disabilities. As appropriate, setting, grouping and individual working can be used to help ensure that individual learning needs are addressed.

Teaching may provide equality of opportunity by enabling the fullest participation of pupils with disabilities in all subjects, as necessary enabling access to the curriculum and learning through aids, adaptations and support. Setting targets for learning involves using the strengths the pupil already has (knowledge, interests, experiences, skills) to improve areas of weakness. The teacher may use an interest in, say, sport or travel by providing reading materials that reflect these interests.

Overcoming potential barriers to learning and assessment

Overcoming potential barriers to learning and assessment for individuals and groups of pupils includes the provision that curriculum planning and assessment take account of the extent and type of difficulty experienced by a pupil. This may involve greater differentiation of tasks and materials, access to specialist equipment and approaches or to alternative or adapted activities, and working closely with others (QCA/DfEE, 1999a: 33–4; 1999b: 35–6). Specific action to provide access to learning for pupils with SEN includes:

1. providing for pupils needing help with communication, language and literacy;
2. planning to develop pupils' understanding through the use of all senses and experiences;
3. planning for the full participation of pupils in learning and in physical and practical activities;
4. helping pupils to manage their behaviour, participate in learning safely and effectively and, as appropriate, prepare for work;
5. helping pupils to manage their emotions and to take part in learning.

In point three above, the apparent separation of 'learning' and 'physical and practical activities' may be unhelpful. Physical and practical activities are, after all, important ways of learning.

The guidance goes on to suggest that providing for pupils needing help with communication, language and literacy can involve using different formats for visual and written materials such as Braille, signs and symbols, and amanuenses. Planning to develop pupils' understanding through the use of all senses and experiences can include encouraging pupils to widen their experiences through play, drama and class visits. Planning for the full participation of pupils in learning and in physical and practical activities can involve using aids and special equipment, adapting tasks and providing support from others. Assisting pupils to manage their behaviour, to participate in learning safely and effectively and, as appropriate, to prepare for work can embrace positive behaviour management, encouraging and teaching independent work skills and teaching safety rules. Helping pupils to manage their emotions and to take part in learning might include selecting tasks and materials to avoid placing unnecessary stress on the pupil. For pupils with disabilities (who may not have SEN), specific actions include planning appropriate time to allow tasks to be completed (QCA/DfEE, 1999a: 34–5; 1999b: 36–7).

Curriculum time

The provision of a broad and balanced curriculum (including the NC) emphasises the flexibility that might be necessary for some pupils, including those with SEN. If a pupil's SEN is mainly related to speech and language difficulties, the curriculum might focus in breadth and in depth to a greater degree than is usual on the development of language and communication skills. Should a pupil's SEN relate to emotional and behavioural difficulties, the curriculum can place particular importance on aspects of subjects (and other provision) that allow the expression and interpretation of emotions, such as art. One way of achieving this is by allocating more time to these areas of the curriculum, within timetabling practicalities. To improve learning generally, particular importance tends to be placed on the 'access' subjects of English, mathematics and information and communication technology.

Section 178 of the Education Act 2002 amends the Learning and Skills Act 2000 to allow funding to be used to provide education and training in the workplace for pupils aged 14–16 years. The Education Act 2002 also extends the definition of secondary education to include education that is received partly at school and partly at another institution. While this is not intended exclusively for pupils with SEN, it is a possible mechanism to help, for example, maintain the motivation of some disaffected pupils who may have emotional and behavioural difficulties.

Schools may set aside aspects of the NC for individual pupils to allow them to implement a wider range of work-related learning programmes. Programmes of study in two NC subjects from science, design and technology and modern foreign languages may be set aside. However, the school

must make arrangements for the pupil to have an interview for careers education before his or her work-related learning programme starts. A curriculum
plan must also be prepared following discussion with the pupil and his or her
parents as well as an induction programme.

Work-related learning programmes can include General National
Vocational Qualification studies or courses provided by a local college of further education, local training providers or community groups. There are also
programmes offering the pupil the chance to sample the working environment and work experiences.

Outside usual curriculum time, many schools offer a range of educational
activities. These include lunchtime clubs, after-school homework clubs and
vacation 'schools', such as summer schools for improving literacy. Where
such activities are voluntary and open to all, the school will want to ensure
that pupils with SEN who would benefit are given every encouragement to
do so. Attendance at such activities may be analysed according to whether or
not the pupils have SEN. Also informative are analyses according to gender, ethnicity and social background and how these combine with SEN (Farrell, 2001).

Disapplication and modification

A maintained school must provide access to the NC for all pupils on its register, including those being temporarily taught at home, in a hospital school or
in a pupil referral unit. However, if it is not possible to offer a pupil the full
NC, aspects can be disapplied. Disapplication and modification may apply to
a programme of study, an attainment target, to assessment, to any any other
components of the NC and to any combination of these, including entire
subjects or the whole NC.

There are two forms of disapplication and modification. The first comes
under s. 18 of the Education Reform Act 1988, which allows some or all of
the NC to be modified or disapplied by a child's statement of SEN. The
second way is through s. 19 of the Act, which states that some or all of the
NC may be temporarily disapplied for a child. Such disapplication can be
considered, for example, for a child whose emotional or physical circumstances are such that it is considered unsuitable that he or she participates in
the full NC. Under s. 19, headteachers can make two types of temporary disapplication: general or special directions. General directions are for children
who do not have a statement of SEN or who do not require a statement but
for whom temporary disapplication is needed. Special directions are for children who may need a statement or who are undergoing the process of having
a statement made (DfES, 1989).

Co-operative learning

Co-operative learning can assist the inclusion in the classroom of a diverse
pupil gouping. Studies on inclusive provision for pupils with SEN were

reviewed by Cross and Walker-Knight (1997). Davidson (1994: 272) identified the attributes that are associated with co-operative learning approaches, and these were elaborated by Cross and Walker-Knight (1997) as follows:

- Common tasks or learning activities suitable for group work: the teacher stuctures a task/activity (of which all group members are aware), to accomplish as a group.
- Small-group learning: groups of two to six pupils are organised by the teacher.
- Co-operative behaviour: teachers directly teach pupils the skills they need to work and learn together.
- Positive independence: the teacher structures a task (perhaps using a team-scoring approach) so the pupils recognise they can attain their goal only by working together.
- Individual responsibility and accountability: pupils are considered individually responsible for the learning that takes place in the group.

Assessment and accreditation flexibility/differentiation

Inclusive assessment

Integral to the NC is a structure of assessment reflecting the approach of the NC itself. An equivalent concept relating to assessment that parallels the inclusive curriculum is that of a more inclusive assessment framework seeking to embrace as many pupils as practicable.

It will be remembered that one of the aspects of the principle of inclusion concerning 'responding to pupils' diverse learning needs' was that the teacher should involve pupils by 'using appropriate assessment approaches' (QCA/DfEE, 1999a: 33; 1999b: 35). An example is assessment that allows the pupil the chance to demonstrate competence and attainment, such as allowing extra time in examination for pupils with difficulties in processing information.

The TTA standards and assessment

The Teacher Training Agency standards, such as the *National Special Education Needs Specialist Standards* (TTA, 1999) and the standards applying to SENCOs (TTA, 1998a) and headteachers (TTA, 1998b), create a framework supportive to SEN provision.

Within this framework, teachers with specialist knowledge, understanding and skills are, for example, expected to be able to take account of the strengths and limitations of different forms of assessment. They are expected to use effectively more specialised informal and formal assessment techniques and use the resulting information to plan and deliver any 'special modes of teaching and support' (TTA, 1999: 10b). They will collate and present the educational implications of multidisciplinary assessments 'to inform curricular decisions'. The teacher will be familiar with assessment procedures that apply to externally validated qualifications and NC assessment, and know how to gain access to the specified special arrangements for pupils with SEN (ibid.: 10b).

Guidelines and the P-scales

Guidelines have been published for planning, teaching and assessing the curriculum for pupils aged between 5 and 16 with learning difficulties (QCA/DfEE, 2001b). This includes pupils who are unlikely to achieve at level 2 of the NC at Key Stage 4 and those who may be working at age-related expectations in some subjects but are well below these in others. The guidelines contain support on developing and planning the curriculum and on developing skills across the curriculum, and subject materials on planning, teaching and assessing each NC subject (religious education, personal, social and health education, and citizenship). The guidelines include descriptions of pupils' attainment that show progress to level 1 of the NC, which may be used to demonstrate attainment and to structure teaching.

As an example of performance indicators, the P-scales (or differentiated performance criteria), are an important assessment tool. Schools that previously set zero-rated targets had to set their first measurable pupil performance targets by December 2001 (for 2003) at the relevant key stage, using the P-scales or other performance criteria (DfEE, 2001e).

Criteria were published in 2001 that provided descriptions of attainment leading to levels 1 and 2 of the NC for English and mathematics, and descriptions leading to level 1 in science (DfEE, 2001e). An earlier document included scales for personal and social development (DfEE, 1998d). A series of documents concerned with pupils with 'learning difficulties' (e.g. DfEE, 2001f) contained subject materials on planning, teaching and assessing each NC subject. These included descriptions of pupil's attainment indicating progress up to level 1 of the NC (see also Berger, 2001).

Key Stage 4

Accreditation relates to developments in the curriculum at Key Stage 4. In England, the QCA sets out the standards that qualifications must meet and the authority uses these to help it decide which qualifications are allowed into the national qualifications framework. The QCA also checks that awarding bodies assess their qualifications correctly. These include entry-level qualifications below level 1.

Within Key Stage 4, pupils with SEN may receive additional support when they complete formal assessments. Schools apply for special arrangements for individual pupils. This might include additional time or a scribe (Joint Council of National Awarding Bodies, annually). The point of special arrangements is to reduce the impact of the pupil's SEN on the process of assessment, not to give unfair advantage.

Disapplication and modification of assessment

This chapter has already described the ways in which, when it is not possible to offer a pupil the full NC, aspects can be disapplied. It will be remembered that disapplication and modification may apply to aspects of assessment – that is, to an attainment target and to assessment as well as to programmes of study (DES, 1989).

School organisation flexibility

In and out-of-class support

The curriculum and the way the school and groups within it are organised must be mutually supportive. The proportion of in and out-of-class support is an important aspect of school organisation. A sensible approach is to seek a balance between the two with a clear rationale and careful monitoring of the impact. The degree of support available is related to the funding that is allocated to it. Such funding comes from the school's formula funding as well as funds that are allocated to pupils with statements of SEN. This translates into support staffing.

The day-to-day responsibility for allocating this support for SEN is often that of the SENCO, given that he or she has an overview of the progress, attainments and requirements of pupils with SEN. Similarly, the management of the support staff and the monitoring of their work and the progress of pupils also rest with the SENCO. Some pupils with emotional and behavioural difficulties that involve concentration may respond better to some work in a quiet area outside the classroom. Similarly, pupils who are disruptive may work better outside class while, at the same time, allowing other pupils to work without disturbance. But in such instances schools may wish to consider developing a clear programme of monitoring out-of-class time with a view gradually to reducing it and increasing the time with other pupils so as to enable other pupils to work unhindered.

Of course, the extent of interaction with the rest of the class should be monitored for pupils with SEN who work within the classroom to help ensure they are a real part of the class and not just physically present. An important factor in this is the progress made by pupils who are withdrawn and who are supported within the class group. If the SENCO monitors this, judgements can be made pragmatically according to progress and improvements in the standards of pupil achievement, including progress in personal and social development.

Pupil groupings

Broad decisions may be made about the grouping of all pupils that effect those pupils with SEN. Pupils may, for example, be placed in 'sets' for part of the day for particular lessons. Decisions concerning those sets to do with group size and staffing ratio will indicate what the school is seeking to do. Is it spreading its resources fairly evenly across sets? Is it providing extra support to pupils with SEN or extra support to pupils who are very able, or both? Is it giving extra support to pupils on the cusp of achieving nationally recognised NC levels that will show up favourably in league tables?

Of course, pupils who have been identified as having SEN will receive some extra support, especially if they have a statement where this will be specified. Important questions are whether any further support is provided over and above this through the school's organisation, whether the school's organisation is the main vehicle for providing that support or whether the school's organisation is aimed more (or equally) at supporting others, such as 'on the cusp' pupils.

The outreach function of special schools and continuing professional development

Further flexibility is provided by effective work across organisations – between mainstream and special schools. This includes special schools offering outreach provision and learning from the knowledge and skills of mainstream teachers, training for mainstream staff and hands-on work with pupils with particular difficulties. This is co-ordinated within the framework of the mainstream school's continuing professional development (see Case Study 12.2).

Case Study 12.2 *Exhall Grange School, Warwickshire*

Exhall Grange School is special school and centre for pupils with sensory and physical disabilities that has beacon status. It supports primary, secondary and special schools in planning, information and communication technology, curriculum issues and other matters to encourage the inclusion of pupils with complex SEN. The school contributes to courses for newly qualified teachers and for the postgraduate certificate in education. Exhall Grange also provides training and practical experience for teachers and teaching assistants working in mainstream schools with pupils who have sensory or/and physical difficulties.

Source: DfES (2002d: 4).

The National Special Educational Needs Specialist Standards (TTA, 1999) also give an indication of approaches to the curriculum and assessment appropriate to pupils with SEN. The standards are for use with teachers and managers in support services; teachers and managers in special classes and units in mainstream schools; special schools and pupil referral units; and headteachers and teachers in mainstream schools.

The intention is that education in mainstream schools is to become more inclusive, which implies (among other things) that it will provide for pupils with increasingly severe and complex SEN. As this evolves, teachers in mainstream schools will increasingly require greater knowledge and skills to provide for these pupils, to the extent that such skills and knowledge are beyond those of good teaching generally. Among the ways of providing the necessary expertise is specialist training provided by the LEA or others. Special schools also offer a range of support, advice, training and hands-on experience. Such development is shaped and monitored through the structure of continuing professional development in the mainstream school.

Individual education plans

Individual education plans (IEPs) – effectively deployed – support curriculum and assessment and organisational flexibility by helping ensure that provision and assessment take place that relate to activities that are additional to or different from what is usual. The knowledge, skills and understanding with which the IEP is concerned are provided through activities additional to or different from those provided for all pupils through the differentiated curriculum. Guidance is provided on IEPs in the *SEN Toolkit* (DfES, 2001f).

Essentially, as a planning tool, the IEP sets out what should be taught (knowledge, skills and understanding), how it should be taught and how often. It also sets out the differentiated steps and the teaching requirements needed to help the pupil reach the IEP learning targets. As an assessment tool, the IEP specifies when the plan is to be reviewed so that progress can be monitored systematically in a formal as well as an ongoing way. IEPs are used to plan interventions through Early Years Action and School Action and through Early Years Action Plus and School Action Plus and for pupils with statements. A way of ensuring a more inclusive approach to IEPs is to consider them as part of the target setting that takes place for every pupil in the school, irrespective of whether the pupil has SEN. In such cases, some pupils with a statement of SEN would be considered to be provided for through the use of whole-school targets.

Not all professionals value IEPs, as a survey of SENCOs in Cornwall indicated (Lingard, 2001). When asked to respond to the statement, 'Children at my school would learn just as effectively without IEPs', twenty agreed, six were not sure and only one disagreed. Asked to respond to the statement, 'IEPs, in themselves, have little impact on improving learning', nineteen agreed, six did not know and none disagreed. When asked to express a view on the statement, 'target setting is problematic because it is extremely difficult to predict how much progress a child will make', fifteen agreed, three did not know and only six disagreed.

The last response (target setting) offers a way to improve the credibility of IEPs. One of the most important features of an IEP is that it should 'raise achievement for pupils with SEN' (DfES, 2001f: 1). Yet the extent to which achievement can be raised is not always clear. Targets are supposed to be specific, measurable, achievable, relevant and time bound (SMART) but also increasingly challenging (ibid.: 3). But it is difficult, even for experienced teachers, to know whether the IEP targets strike the right balance between being challenging and realistic.

This situation will change as more schools and LEAs develop the use of such assessments as the P-scales. As assessments for pupils with SEN become more embedded in school procedures, it becomes more practicable to set whole SEN cohort targets and compare these with other similar cohorts of pupils. This allows benchmarks to be used for value-added purposes as schools compare their performance with schools that have similar cohorts of pupils with SEN. This in turn enables SENCOs and others to relate IEP targets for individual pupils to those to which the school is aspiring for the whole cohort of pupils with SEN. In brief, a similar process to that which is presently used to raise the standards of pupils who do not have SEN will be used for pupils with SEN.

Thinking points

Practitioners may wish to consider:

■ the extent to which the school's present SEN policy reflects the intention to include pupils with a wide range of SEN and raise their attainment;
■ the extent to which, in their local schools, IEP targets reflect the overarching targets for whole cohorts of pupils with SEN; and
■ the degree to which they are clear about what represents inclusive practice in lessons, differentiation, planning, assessment and other features of education.

▌Key text

Department for Education and Skills (DfES) (2001) *Inclusive Schooling: Children with Special Educational Needs*. London: DfES.
This document offers guidance on the legal framework for inclusive schooling.

References

Aarons, M. and Gittens, T. (1992) *The Handbook of Autism: A Guide for Parents and Professionals*. London: Routledge.

Ainscow, M. (1988) 'Beyond the eyes of the monster: an analysis of recent trends in assessment and recording', *Support for Learning*, 3 (3): 149–53.

Ainscow, M. (1995) 'Education for all: making it happen', *Support for Learning*, 10 (4): 147–54.

Allen, J. (1996) 'Foucault and special educational needs: a "box of tools" for analysing children's experiences of mainstreaming', *Disability and Society*, 11 (2): 219–33.

Allen, J., Brown, S. and Riddell, S. (1998) 'Permission to speak? Theorising special education inside the classroom', in C. Clarke *et al.* (eds) *Theorising Special Education*. London: Routledge.

All Party Parliamentary Group on Autism (2001) *The Rising Challenge*. London: APPGA.

American Psychiatric Association (1994) *Diagnostic and Statistical Manual of Mental Disorders* (4th. edn). Washington, DC: American Psychiatric Association.

Andrews, A. (1988) 'Conversation', *Journal of the British Association of Teachers of the Deaf*, 12 (2): 29–32.

Audit Commission (2002) *Special Educational Needs: A Mainstream Issue-briefing*. London, Audit Commission.

Bailey, J. (1998) 'Medical and psychological models in special needs education', in C. Clark, *et al.* (eds) *Theorising Special Education*. London: Routledge.

Baillargeon, R. and DeVos, J. (1991) 'Object permanence in young infants: further evidence', *Child Development*, 62: 1227–46.

Baker, C. (1993) *Foundations of Bilingual Education and Bilingualism*. Clevedon: Multilingual Matters.

Baker, R. and Knight, P. (1998) '"Total communication' current policy', in S. Gregory *et al.* (eds) *Issues in Deaf Education*. London: David Fulton.

Ball, M. (2002) *Getting Sure Start Started*. London: Department for Education and Skills.

Balshaw, M.H. (1999) *Help in the Classroom*. London: David Fulton.

Barker, P. (1998) *Michel Foucault: An Introduction*. Edinburgh: Edinburgh University Press.

Barnes, C. and Mercer, G. (1996) *Exploring the Divide: Illness and Disability*. Leeds: Disability Press.

Barnes, C. Mercer, G. and Shakespeare, T. (1999) *Exploring Disability: A Sociological Introduction*. Cambridge: Polity Press.

Bayliss, P. (1998) 'Models of complexity: theory-driven intervention practices', in C. Clark *et al.* (eds) *Theorising Special Education*. London: Routledge.

Beek, C. (2002) 'The distribution of resources to support inclusive learning', *Support for Learning*, 17 (1).

Berger, A. (ed.) (2001) *Assessing Pupil's Performance Using the P Levels*. London: David Fulton.

Berger, A., Henderson, J. and Morris, D. (1999) *Implementing the Literacy Hour for Pupils with Learning Difficulties*. London: David Fulton.

Berger, P. and Luckmann, T. (1971) *The Social Construction of Reality*. Harmondsworth: Penguin Books.

Bender, R. (1970) *The Conquest of Deafness*. Cleveland OH: Case Western Reserve University Press.

Bhaskar, R. (1986) *Scientific Realism and Human Emancipation*. London: Verso.

Bibby, P. and Lunt, I. (1996) *Working for Children: Securing Provision for Children with Special Educational Needs*. London: David Fulton.

Booth, T. (1998) 'The poverty of special education: theories to the rescue?', in C. Clark *et al.* (eds) *Theorising Special Education*. London: Routledge.

Booth, T., Ainscow, M., Black-Hawkins, K., Vaughn, M. and Shaw, L. (2000) *Index for Inclusion: Developing Learning and Participation in Schools*. Bristol: Centre for Studies in Inclusive Education.

British Psychological Society (1999) *Dyslexia, Literacy and Psychological Assessment: Report by a Working Party of the Division of Educational and Child Psychology of the British Psychological Society*. Leicester: BPS.

Brooks, G. (2002) *What Works for Children with Learning Difficulties? The Effectiveness of Intervention Schemes*. London: Department for Education and Skills.

Bryant, P.E. and Trabasso, T. (1971) 'Transitive inferences and memory in young children', *Nature*, 232: 456–8.

Campbell, J. and Oliver, M. (1996) *Disability Politics: Understanding our Past, Changing our Future*. London: Routledge.

Campbell, M. and Cueva, J.E. (1995) 'Psychopharmacology in child and adolescent psychiatry: review of the past seven years', *Journal of the American Academy of Child and Adolescent Psychiatry*, 34: 1262–72.

Carnine, D.W. and Silbert, J. (1979) *Direct Instruction Reading*. Columbus, OH: Charles E. Merrill.

Cavanagh, M. (2002) *Against Equality of Opportunity*. Oxford: Oxford University Press.

Chappell, A.L. (1998) 'Still out in the cold: people with learning difficulties and the social model of disability', in T. Shakespeare (ed.) *The Disability Reader: Social Science Perspectives*. London: Cassell.

Cheu, J. (2002) 'De-gene-erates, replicants and other aliens: (re)defining disability in futuristic film', in M. Corker and T, Shakespeare (eds) *Disability/post-modernity: Embodying Disability Theory*. London: Continuum.

Chewning, B. and Sleath, B. (1996) 'Medication decision-making and management: a client centred model', *Social Science Medicine*, 42 (3): 389–98.

Clark, C., Dyson, A. and Millward, A. (1998) 'Theorising special education: time to move on?', in C. Clark *et al.* (eds) *Theorising Special Education*. London: Routledge.

Clark, C., Dyson, A., Millward, A. and Robson, S. (1999) 'Theories of inclusion, theories of schools: deconstructing and reconstructing the inclusive school', *British Educational Research Journal*, 25 (2): 157–77.

Clark, T. (2003) *Public Service Agreements at the Local Level Education. Management Information Exchange Report* 70. Slough: National Foundation of Educational Research.

Cole, T. (1989) *Apart or A Part? Integration and the Growth of British Special Education*. Milton Keynes: Open University Press.

Cooper, P. (1993) *Effective Schools for Disaffected Students*. London: Routledge.

Cooper, P. and Ideus, K. (1995) 'Is attention deficit hyperactivity disorder a Trojan horse?', *Support for Learning*, 10 (1): 29–33.

Corbett, J. (1996) *Bad-mouthing: The Language of Special Educational Needs*. London: Falmer Press.

Corbett, J. (1998) *Special Educational Needs: A Cultural Analysis*. London: Cassell.

Cross, L. and Walker-Knight, D. (1997) 'Inclusion: developing collaborative and co-operative school communities,' *The Education Forum*, 61: 269–77.

Crow, L. (1996) 'Including all of our lives: renewing the social model of disability', in C. Barnes and G. Mercer (eds) *Exploring the Divide: Illness and Disabilty*. Leeds: The Disability Press.

Cunningham, C. and Davies, H. (1985) *Working with Parents: Framework for Collaboration*. Buckingham: Open University Press.

Davidson, N. (1994) 'Co-operative and collaborative learning: an integrative perspective', in J.S. Thousand *et al.* (eds) *Creativity and Collaborative Learning: A Practical Guide for Empowering Students and Teachers*. Baltimore, MD:, P.H. Brookes.

Denton, D. (1976) 'The philosophy of total communication', *Supplement to British Deaf News*. Carlisle: British Deaf Association.

Department for Education (1994) *The Code of Practice on the Identification and Assessment of Special Educational Needs*. London: DfE.

Department for Education and Employment (DfEE) (1995) *Secondary School Performance Tables*. London: DfEE.

Department for Education and Employment (1996) *Secondary School Performance Tables*. London: DfEE.

Department for Education and Employment (1997a) *Excellence for All Children: Meeting Special Educational Needs*. London: DfEE.

Department for Education and Employment (1997b) *Excellence in Schools*. London: DfEE.

Department for Education and Employment (1998a) *The National Literacy Strategy: A Framework for Teaching*. London: DfEE.

Department for Education and Employment (1998b) *Meeting Special Educational Needs: A Programme for Action*. London: DfEE.

Department for Education and Employment (1998c) *Fair Funding: Improving Delegation to Schools, Consultation Paper*. London: DfEE.

Department for Education and Employment (1998d) *Supporting the Target Setting Process: Guidance for Effective target Setting for Pupils with Special Educational Needs*, London: DfEE.

Department for Education and Employment (1999a) *The National Numeracy Strategy: Framework for Teaching Mathematics from Reception to Year 6*. London: DfEE.

Department for Education and Employment (1999b) *Circular 10/99*. London: DfEE.

Department for Education and Employment (1999c) *Circular 11/99*. London: DfEE.

Department for Education and Employment (2000a) *A Guide to the Law for School Governors – Community Schools*. London: DfES.

Department for Education and Employment (2000b) *A Guide to the Law for School Governors – Foundation Schools*. London: DfES.

Department for Education and Employment (2000c) *A Guide to the Law for School Governors – Voluntary Aided Schools*. London: DfES.

Department for Education and Employment (2000d) *A Guide to the Law for School Governors – Voluntary Controlled Schools*. London: DfES.

Department for Education and Employment (2000e) *Governors' Annual Reports and School Prospectuses in Primary Schools*. London: DfES.

Department for Education and Employment (2000f) *Governors' Annual Reports and School Prospectuses in Secondary Schools*. London: DfES.

Department for Education and Employment (2000g) *The Role of the Local Education Authority in School Education*. London: DfEE.

Department for Education and Employment (2000h) *SEN Code of Practice on the Assessment of Pupils with Special Educational Needs and SEN Thresholds: Good Practice Guidance on Identification and Provision for Pupils with Special Educational Needs*. London: DfEE.

Department for Education and Employment (2001a) *The Key Stage 3 National Strategy: Literacy Across the Curriculum*. London: DfEE.

Department for Education and Employment (2001b) *The Key Stage 3 National Strategy: Numeracy Across the Curriculum Notes for School Based Training*. London: DfEE.

Department for Education and Employment (2001c) *Departmental Report March 2001*. London: DfEE.

Department for Education and Employment (2001d) *Code of Practice on Local Education Authority and School Relationships*. London: DfEE.

Department for Education and Employment (2001e) *Supporting the Target Setting Process: Guidance for Effective Target Setting for Pupils with Special Educational Needs*. London: DfEE.

Department for Education and Employment (2001f) *Planning, Teaching and Assessing the Curriculum for Pupils with Learning Difficulties: General Guidelines*. London: DfEE.

Department for Education and Employment/Department of Health (DfEE/DoH) (2000) *Provision of Speech and Language Services to Children with Special Educational Needs: Report of the Working Group*. London: DfEE/DoH.

Department of Education and Science (DfES) (1978) *Special Educational Needs: Report of the Committee of Enquiry into the Education of Handicapped Children and Young People* (the Warnock Report). London: HMSO.

Department for Education and Science (1989) *Circular 15/89: Temporary Exceptions from the National Curriculum*. London: DfES.

Department for Education and Skills (2001a) *Special Educational Needs Code of Practice*. London: DfES.

Department for Education and Skills (2001b) *Schools Achieving Success*. London: DfES.

Department for Education and Skills (2001c) *The Distribution of Resources to Support Inclusion*. London: DfEE.

Department for Education and Skills (2001d) *The National Numeracy Strategy: Towards the National Curriculum for Mathematics: Examples of what Pupils with Special Educational Needs should be Able to Do at Each P Level*. London: DfES.

Department for Education and Skills (2001e) *Inclusive Schooling: Children with Special Educational Needs*. London: DfES.

Department for Education and Skills (2001f) *SEN Toolkit – Section 5: Managing Individual Education Plans*. London: DfES.

Department for Education and Skills (2002a) *Best Value in Schools*. London: DfEE.

Department for Education and Skills (2002b) *Fair Funding: An Explanatory Guide*. London: DfEE.

Department for Education and Skills (2002c) *Statistics of Education, Special Educational Needs in England: January 2002 Issue No. 10/02 November 2002*. London: HMSO.

Department for Education and Skills (2002d) *Special Educational Needs Update 9 June 2002*. London: DfES.

Department for Education and Skills (2002e) *Excellence in Cities: Schools Extending Excellence Annual Report 2000–2001*. London: DfES.

Department for Education and Skills (2002f) *Developing the Role of School Support Staff: The Consultation*. London: DfES.

Department for Education and Skills (2003) *Report of the Special Schools Working Group*. London: HMSO.

Department for Education and Skills/Department of Health (DfES/DoH) (2002a) *Autistic Spectrum Disorders: Good Practice Guidance: 01Pointers to Good Practice*. London: DfES/DoH.

Department for Education and Skills/Department of Health (2002b) *Autistic Spectrum Disorders Good Practice Guidance: 02 Pointers to Good Practice*. London: DfES/DoH.

Department of Health (DoH) (2002) *Abortion Statistics*. London: DoH.

Department of Health/Department for Education and Skills (DoH/DfES) (2000) *Provision of Speech and Language Therapy Services to Children with Special Educational Needs (England): Report of the Working Group November 2000*. London: DoH/DfEE.

Dessent, A. (1996) *Options for Partnership between Health, Education and Social Services*. Tamworth: National Association for Special Educational Needs.

Dewey, J. (1899/1976) 'The school and society', in J.A. Boydston (ed.) *John Dewey: The Middle Works 1899–1924. Vol. 1*. Carbondale, IL: Southern Illinois University Press.

Disability Rights Commission (2001a) *A Disability Code of Practice (Schools)*. London: DRC.

Disability Rights Commission (2001b) *A Disability Code of Practice (post 16)*. London: DRC.

Dockerell, J. and McShane, J. (1993) *Children's Learning Difficulties: A Cognitive Approach*. Oxford: Blackwell.

Donellan, C. (2000) *The Abortion Issue: Issues Vol. 34*. Cambridge: Independence Educational Publishers.

Drake, R. (1996) 'A critique of the role of traditional charities', in L. Barton (ed.) *Disability and Society: Emerging Issues and Insights*. London: Longman.

Elliot, J. and Place, M. (1998) *Children in Difficulty: A Guide to Understanding and Helping*. London: Routledge.

English, A., Essex, J. and the West Midlands SEN Regional Partnership (2001) *Report on Autistic Spectrum Disorders: A Comprehensive Report into Identification, Training and Provision Focusing on the Needs of Children and Young People with an Autistic Spectrum Disorder and their Families within the West Midlands Region* (www.westmidlandsrcp.org.uk).

English, V. and Sommerville, A. (2002) 'Drawing the line: the need for balance', in E. Lee *et al.* (eds) *Designer Babies: Where should we Draw the Line?. Institute of Ideas Debating Matters Series.* London: Hodder & Stoughton.

Evans, P. (2000) 'Evidence-based practice: how will we know what works? An international perspective', in H. Daniel (ed.) *Special Education Re-formed: Beyond Rhetoric?. New Millennium Series.* London: Falmer Press.

Evans, J. and Gerber, M. (2000) 'The changing governance of education', in M.J. McLaughlin and M. Rouse (eds) *Special Education and School Reform in the United States and Great Britain.* London: Routledge.

Farrell, M. (1999) *Key Issues in Primary Schools.* London: Routledge.

Farrell, M. (2001) *Standards and Special Educational Needs.* London: Continuum.

Farrell, M. (2002) *The Special Education Handbook* (3rd end). London: David Fulton.

Farrell, M. (2003) *Understanding Special Educational Needs: A Guide for Student Teachers.* London: Routledge.

Farrell, M., Kerry, T. and Kerry, C. (1995) *The Blackwell Handbook of Education.* Oxford: Blackwell.

Ferguson, P.M. and Ferguson, D.L. (1995) 'The interpretivist view of special education and disability: the value of telling stories', in T.M. Skrtic (ed.) *Disability and Democracy: Reconstructing (Special) Education for Post-modernity.* New York, NY: Teachers College Press.

Fish, J. and Evans, J. (1995) *Managing Special Education: Codes, Charters and Competition.* Buckingham: Open University Press.

Fitzgerald, L. (2000) *Provision for Children with Speech and Language Needs in England and Wales: Facilitating Communication between Education and Health Services.* Nottingham: Department for Education and Employment Publications.

Fletcher, A. (2002) 'Making it better? Disability and genetic choice', in E. Lee *et al.* (eds) *Designer Babies: Where should we Draw the Line?. Institute of Ideas Debating Matters Series.* London: Hodder & Stoughton.

Fletcher-Campbell, F. (2002) 'The financing of special education: lessons from Europe', *Support for Learning*, 17 (1).

Forrester, S. and Stenson, A. (2001) *A Guide to Funding from Government Departments and Agencies* (2nd edn). London: The Directory of Social Change.

Foucault, M. (1977) 'Intellectuals and power: a conversation between Michel Foucault and Giles Deleuze', in D. Bouchard (ed.) *Language, Counter-memory, Practice: Selected Essays and Interviews by Michel Foucault.* Oxford: Blackwell.

Foucault, M. (1982) 'The subject and power', in H. Dreyfus and P. Rabinow (eds) *Michel Foucault: Beyond Structuralism and Hermeneutics.* Brighton: Harvester.

Foxten, T. and McBrien, J. (1981) *Training Staff in Behavioural Methods: Trainee Workbook.* Manchester: Manchster University Press.

Gallimore, R. and Tharpe, R. (1990) 'Teaching mind in society', in L.C. Moll (ed.) *Vigotsky and Education: Instructional Implications and Applications of Sociohistorical Psychology.* Cambridge: Cambridge University Press.

Garner, P. and Davies, J.D. (2001) *Introducing Special Educational Needs: A Companion Guide for Student Teachers.* London: David Fulton.

Gordon, M. (1999) 'Surviving the literacy hour: the way ahead', in M. Minson (ed.) *Surviving the Literacy Hour.* Tamworth, Staffordshire: National Association of Special Educational Needs.

Greenwood, C. (2002) *Understanding the Needs of Parents: Guidelines for Effective Collaboration with Parents of Children with Special Educational Needs.* London: David Fulton.

Gross, J., Berger, A. and Garnett, J. (1999) 'Special needs and the literacy hour: some general principles', in A. Berger and J. Gross (eds) *Teaching the Literacy Hour in an Inclusive Classroom.* London: David Fulton.

Hadley, J. (1996) *Abortion: Between Freedom and Necessity.* London: Virago.

Harris, F. (2002) *The First Implementation of the Sure Start Language Measure*. London: Department of Education and Skills.

Harris, J. (2002) 'Liberation in reproduction', in E. Lee *et al.* (eds) *Designer Babies: Where should we Draw the Line?. Debating Matters Series*. London: Hodder & Stoughton.

Hay McBer (2000) *Research into Teacher Effectiveness: A Model of Teacher Effectiveness*. London: Deprartment for Education and Employment.

Heeks, P. and Kinnell, M. (1997) *Learning Support for Special Educational Needs: Potential for Progress*. London: Taylor Graham.

Heywood, J. (1978) *Children in Care* (3rd edn). London, Routledge & Keegan Paul.

Hornby, G., Atkinson, M. and Howard, J. (1997) *Controversial Issues in Special Education*. London: David Fulton.

House of Commons (1995) *Meeting Special Educational Needs: Statements of Needs and Provision*. London: HMSO.

Howell, K.W., Kaplan, J.S. and O'Connell, C.Y. (1979) *Evaluating Exceptional Children: A Task Analysis Approach*. Columbus, OH: Charles E. Merrill.

Humphrey, J C. (2000) 'Researching disability politics, or some problems with the social model in practice', *Disability and Society*, 15 (1): 63–86.

Humphries, A. and Ramm, S. (1987) 'Autism the isolating syndrome', *Special Children*, 14 October: 16–19.

Hurt, J. (1988) *Outside the Mainstream: A History of Special Education*. London: Batsford.

I-CAN (2001) *Joint Professional Framework for All Teachers and Speech and Language therapists working with Speech, Language and Communication Needs*. London: I-CAN.

International League of Societies for Persons with Mental Handicap (Inclusion International) (1994) *Just Technology? From Principles to Practice in Bioethical Issues*. North York, Ontario: L'Institut Roeher.

Joint Council of National Awarding Bodies (annually) *Assessment in General National Vocational Qualifications: Provision for Candidates with Special Needs*. London: JCNAB.

Kellman, H. (1970) 'The relevance of social research into social issues – problems and pitfalls', *Sociological Review Monograph* 16.

Konner, M. (1993) *The Trouble with Medicine*. London: BBC Books.

Lacey, P. (2000) 'Multidisciplinary work: challenges and possibilities', in H.Daniels (ed.) *Special Education Re-formed: Beyond Rhetoric?. New Millennium Series*. London: Falmer Press.

Lacey, P. and Thomas, J. (1993) *Support Services and the Curriculum*. London: David Fulton.

Lane, H. (1984) *When the Mind Hears: A History of the Deaf*. New York, NY: Random House.

Lauder, H., Jamieson, I. and Wikeley, F. (1998) 'Models of effective schools: limits and capabilities' R. in Slee *et al.* (eds) *School Effectiveness for Whom?*. London: Falmer Press.

Lave, J. and Wenger, E. (1991) 'Practice, person and social world', in J. Lave and E. Wenger (eds) *Situated Learning: Legitimate Peripheral Participation*. Cambridge: Cambridge University Press.

Law, J., Lindsay, G., Peacey, N., Gascoigne, M., Soloff, N., Radford, J. and Band, S. (2001) 'Facilitating communication between education and health services: the provision for children with speech and language needs', *British Journal of Special Education*, 28 (3).

Lee, E. (2002) 'Introduction', in E. Lee *et al.* (eds) *Designer Babies: Where should we Draw the Line?. Institute of Ideas Debating Matters Series*. London: Hodder & Stoughton.

Leeds Local Education Authority (1995) *Deaf and Hearing Impaired Service (DAHISS) Policy Statement*. Leeds: LEA Publications.

Lingard, T. (1996) 'Why our theoretical models of integration are inhibiting effective integration', *Emotional and Behavioural Difficulties*, 1 (2): 39–45.

Lingard, T. (2000) 'Is the National Literacy Strategy raising the achievement of low attainers?', *British Journal of Special Education*, 27 (3): 117–23.

Lingard, T. (2001) 'Does the *Code of Practice* help secondary school SENCOs to improve teaching?', *British Journal of Special Education*, 28 (4): 187–90.

Lipsky, D.K. and Gartner, A. (1996) 'Inclusion, school restructuring and the remaking of American society', *Harvard Educational Review*, 66 (4): 762–95.

Literacy Task Force/Department for Education and Employment (1997) *A Reading Revolution: How We can Teach every Child to Read well, the Preliminary Report Chaired by Michael Barber*. London: LTF/DfEE.

Llewellyn, A. and Hogan, K. (2000) 'The use and abuse of models of disability', *Disability and Society*, 15 (1): 157–65.

Local Government Association, National Health Service Confederation, Association of Directors of Social Services (2002) *Serving Children Well: A New Vision for Children's Services*. London: LGA, NHSC, ADSS.

Lotter, V. (1966) 'Epidemiology of autistic conditions in young children. 1. Prevalence', *Social Psychiatry*, 1: 124–37.

Lunt, I. and Norwich, B. (1999) *Can Effective Schools be Inclusive Schools? (Perspectives on Educational Policy)*. London: Institute of Education.

Lyon, J. (1994) 'Hope for the hyperactive', *The Times Educational Supplement*, 21 October.

McBrien, J., Farrell, P. and Foxten, T. (1992) *Education of the Developmentally Young Trainee Workbook* (2nd edn). Manchester: Manchester University Press.

Mackay, G. (2002) 'The disappearance of disability? Thoughts on a changing culture', *Journal of Special Education*, 29 (4).

Meadows, S. (1988) 'Piaget's contribution to understanding cognitive development: an assessment for the late 1980s', in K. Richardson and S. Sheldon (eds) *Cognitive Development to Adolescence*. Milton Keynes/Hove: Open University/Lawrence Erlbaum Associates.

Meijer, C. (ed.) (1999) *Financing of Special Needs Education: A Seventeen Country Study of the Relationship between Financing of Special Needs Education and Inclusion*. Middelfart: European Agency for Development in Special Needs Education.

Meltzoff, A.N. and Moore, M.K. (1994) 'Imitation, memory and the representation of persons', *Infant Behaviour and Development*, 17: 83–99.

Mittler, P. (2000) *Working towards Inclusive Education*. London: David Fulton.

Mortimore, P. and Sammons, P. (1997) 'End piece: a welcome and reposte to critics', in J. White and M. Barber (eds) *Perspectives on School Effectiveness and School Improvement. Bedford Way Papers*. London: Institute of Education, University of London.

National Deaf Children's Society (1996) *NDCS Directory 1996–7*. London: NDCS.

National Foundation for Educational research (2000) *Who Holds the Purse: Funding Schools to Meet Special Educational Needs*. Slough: NFER.

Norwich, B. (2000) 'Inclusion in education: from concepts, values and critique to practice', in H. Daniels (ed.) *Special Education Re-formed: Beyond Rhetoric?. New Millennium Series*. London: Falmer Press.

Nozick, R. (1974) *Anarchy, State and Utopia*. Oxford: Blackwell.

Office for Standards in Education (OfSTED) (1999a) *Special Education 1994–1998: A Review of Special Schools, Secure Units and Pupil Referral Units in England*. London: HMSO.

Office for Standards in Education (1999b) *Pupils with Specific Learning Difficulties in Mainstream Schools: A Survey of the Provision in Mainstream Primary and Secondary Schools for Pupils with a Statement of Special Educational Needs Relating to Specific Learning Difficulties*. London: OfSTED.

Office for Standards in Education (2000) *Evaluating Educational Inclusion: Guidance for Inspectors and Schools*. London: OfSTED.

Office for Standards in Education (2001) *Improving Inspection, Improving Schools: Consultation on Future Arrangements for School Inspection*. London: OfSTED.

Office for Standards in Education (2002) *Framework for the Inspection of Local Education Authorities*. London: OfSTED.

Office for Standards in Education (2003a) *Inspecting Schools: The Framework*. Norwich: HMSO.

Office for Standards in Education (2003b) *Handbook for Inspecting Primary and Nursery Schools with Guidance on Self Evaluation.* Norwich: HMSO.

Office for Standards in Education (2003c) *Handbook for Inspecting Secondary Schools with Guidance on Self Evaluation.* Norwich: HMSO.

Office for Standards in Education (2003d) *Handbook for Inspecting Special Schools and Pupil Referral Units with Guidance on Self Evaluation.* Norwich: HMSO.

Parsons, T. (1952) *The Social System.* New York, NY: Free Press.

Phtiaka, H. (1998) *Special Kids for Special Treatment? How Special do you Need to be to Find Yourself in a Special School?.* London: Falmer Press.

Piaget, J. (1970) 'Piaget's theory', in P.H. Mussen (ed.) *Manual of Child Psychology.* London: Wiley.

Piaget, J. and Inhelder, B. (1969) *The Psychology of the Child.* London: Routledge & Kegan Paul.

Pritchard, D.G. (1963) *Education of the Handicapped 1760–1960.* London: Routledge & Kegan Paul.

Pumfrey, P. and Mittler, P. (1989) 'Peeling off the label', *The Times Educational Supplement,* 13 October.

Qualification and Curriculum Authority/Department for Education and Employment (QCA/DfEE) (1999a) *The National Curriculum: Handbook for Primary Teachers in England.* London: QCA/DfEE.

Qualifications and Curriculum Authority/Department for Education and Employment (1999b) *The National Curriculum Handbook for Secondary Teachers in England.* London: QCA/DfEE.

Qualifications and Curriculum Authority/Department for Education and Employment (2000) *Curriculum Guidance for the Foundation Stage.* London: QCA/DfEE.

Qualifications and Curriculum Authority/Department for Education and Employment (2001a) *Supporting the Target Setting Process: Guidance for Effective Target Setting for Pupils with Special Educational Needs.* London: QCA/DfEE.

Qualifications and Curriculum Authority/Department for Education and Employment (2001b) *Planning, Teaching and Assessing the Curriculum for Pupils with Learning Difficulties (series).* London: QCA/DfEE.

Ramasut, A. and Reynolds, D. (1993) 'Developing effective whole school approaches to special educational needs: from school effectiveness to school development practice', in R. Slee (ed.) *Is There a Desk with my Name on it? The Politics of Integration.* London: Falmer Press.

Rawls, J. (1971) *A Theory of Justice.* Cambridge, MA: Harvard University Press.

Raybould, E.C. and Solity, J.E. (1998) 'Precision teaching and all that', *British Journal of Special Education,* 1 (1): 32–3.

Reinders, H.S. (2000) *The Future of the Disabled in Liberal Society: An Ethical Analysis.* Notre Dame, IN: University of Notre Dame Press.

R v. London Borough of Harrow ex parte M 8 October 1996.

Safford, P.L. and Safford, E.J. (1996) *A History of Childhood and Disability.* New York, NY: Teachers College Press.

Salovey, P. and Sluyter, D.J. (1997) *Emotional Development and Emotional Intelligence.* New York, NY: Basic Books.

Schools Plus Policy Action Team 11 (2000) *Schools Plus: Building Learning Communities – Improving the Educational Chances of Children and Young People from Disadvantaged Areas.* London: DfEE.

Schreibman, L. (1988) *Autism.* Thousand Oaks, CA: Sage.

Shayer, M., Kuchemann, D.E. and Wylam, H. (1976) 'The distribution of Piagetian stages of thinking in British middle and secondary school children', *British Journal of Educational Psychology* 46: 164–73.

Shayer, M. and Wylam, H. (1978) 'The distribution of Piagetian stages of thinking in British middle and secondary school children. II', *British Journal of Educational Psychology* 48: 162–70.

Skrtic, T. (1991) *Behind Special Education: A Critical Analysis of Professional Culture and School Organisation.* Denver, CO: Love Publications.

Skrtic, T.M. (1995a) 'The functionalist view of special education and disability: deconstructing the conventional knowledge tradition', in T.M. Skrtic (ed.) *Disability and Democracy: Reconstructing (Special) Education for Post-modernity*. New York, NY: Teachers College Press.

Skrtic, T.M. (1995b) *Disability and Democracy: Reconstructing (Special) Education for Post-modernity*. New York, NY: Teachers College Press.

Sleeter, C.E. (1995) 'Radical structural perspectives on the creation and use of learning disabilities', in T.M. Skrtic (ed.) *Disability and Democracy: Reconstructing (Special) Education for Post-modernity*. New York, NY: Teachers College Press.

Smith, P.K. and Cowrie, H. (1991) *Understanding Children's Development* (2nd edn). Oxford: Blackwell.

Solity, J.E. and Raybould, E. (1988) *A Teacher's Guide to Special Needs: A Positive Response to the 1981 Act*. Milton Keynes: Open University Press.

Special Educational Needs and Disability Tribunal (2002) *Annual Report 2001–2002*. London: SENDIST.

Special Educational Needs Tribunal (2000) *Annual Report 1999–2000*. London: SEN Tribunal.

Special Educational Needs Tribunal (2001) *How to Appeal*. London: SEN Tribunal.

Stoll, L. and Mortimore, P. (1997) 'School effectiveness and school improvement,' in J. White and M. Barber (eds) *Perspectives on School Effectiveness and School Improvement. Bedford Way Papers*. London: Institute of Education, University of London.

Teacher Training Agency (TTA) (1998a) *National Standards for Special Educational Needs Co-ordinators*. London: TTA.

Teacher Training Agency (1998b) *The National Standards for Headteachers*. London: TTA.

Teacher Training Agency (1999) *National Special Educational Needs Specialist Standards*. London: TTA.

Teacher Training Agency (2000) *Using the National Standards for Special Educational Needs Co-ordinators (SENCOs)*. London: TTA.

Teacher Training Agency (2002a) *Qualifying to Teach: Professional Standards for Qualified Teacher Status and Requirements for Initial Teacher Training*. London: TTA.

Teacher Training Agency (2002b) *Induction Standards (Draft Proposals for September 2002)*. London: TTA.

Thomas, G. (1997) *Exam Performance in Special Schools*. Bristol: Bristol Centre for Studies on Inclusive Education.

Thomas, R.M. (1985) *Comparing Theories of Child Development* (2nd edn). Belmont, CA: Wadsworth.

Tizzard, J. (2002) '"Designer babies": the case for choice', in E. Lee *et al.* (eds) *Designer Babies: Where should we Draw the Line? Institute of Ideas Debating Matters Series*. London: Hodder & Stoughton.

Tomlinson, S. (1982) *A Sociology of Special Education*. London: Routledge & Kegan Paul.

Tomlinson, S. (1995) 'The radical structuralist view of special education and disability: unpopular perspectives on their origins and development', in T.M. Skrtic (ed.) *Disability and Democracy: Reconstructing (Special) Education for Post-modernity*. New York, NY: Teachers College Press.

Tomlinson-Keasey, C. (1978) 'The structure of concrete operational thought', *Child Development*, 50: 1153–63.

Tunstill, J., Allnock, D., Meadows, P. and McLeod, A. (2002) *Early Experiences of Implementing Sure Start*. London: DfES.

United Nations (1993) *The Rights of the Child* Department of Health; Children's Rights Development Unit, New York.

United Nations Educational, Scientific and Cultural Organisation (UNESCO) (1994) *The Salamanca Statement and Framework for Action on Special Needs Education*. Paris: UNESCO.

United Nations Educational, Scientific and Cultural Organisation (1996) *Survey on Special Needs Education Law*. Paris: UNESCO.

Van Uden, A. (1977) *A World of Language for Deaf Children*. Lisse, the Netherlands: Swets & Zeitlinger.

Vygotsky, L.S. (1978) *Mind in Society: The Development of Psychological Processes*. Cambridge, MA: Harvard University Press.

Vygotsky, L.S. (1987) 'Thinking and speech,' in R.W. Reiber and A.S. Carton (eds) *The Collected Works of L.S. Vygotsky. Volume 1. Problems of General Psychology*. London. Plenum Press.

Warnock, Baroness M. (1993) 'The problem of knowledge,' in B. Holland and C. Kyriacou (eds) *Genetics and Society*. Wokingham: Addison-Wesley.

Watson, L. (1998) 'Oralism – current policy and practice' in S. Gregory *et al.* (eds) *Issues in Deaf Education*. London. David Fulton.

Wearmouth, J. (2000) *Special Educational Provision: Meeting the Challenges in Schools*. London: Hodder & Stoughton Educational/Open University.

Weber, M. (1972) 'Selections on education and politics', in B. Cosin (ed.) *Education Structure and Society*. Harmondsworth: Penguin Books.

White, M. and Cameron, S. (1987) *Portage Early Education Programme*. Windsor: NFER-Nelson.

Wing, L. and Gould, J. (1979) 'Severe impairments of social interaction and associated abnormalities in children: epidemiology and classification', *Journal of Autism and Developmental Disorders*, 9: 11–29.

Wodrich, D.L. (1994) *Attention Deficit Hyperactivity Disorder: What every Parent Wants to Know*. London, Paul Brooks.

Woods, P. (1979) *The Divided School*. London: Routledge & Kegan Paul.

World Health Organisation (2001) *ICF – International Classification of Functioning, Disability and Health*. Geneva: WHO.

Worthington, A. (ed.) (2000) *The Fulton Special Education Digest: Selected Resources for Teachers, Parents and Carers*. London: David Fulton.

Index